SQL FUNCTIONS DICTIONARY

Unlocking the Power of SQL

Kiet Huynh

Table of Contents

Introduction

Welcome to "SQL Functions Dictionary: Unlocking the Power of SQL." In the ever-evolving world of data management and analysis, SQL (Structured Query Language) remains a cornerstone of the field. One of SQL's most versatile and valuable features is its extensive collection of functions, designed to assist you in manipulating and extracting meaningful insights from your data.

This comprehensive reference guide is your gateway to mastering the diverse array of SQL functions. Whether you're a novice database administrator or an experienced data analyst, you'll find invaluable resources in this book. We've compiled a rich compendium of SQL functions, each carefully detailed with its syntax, usage, and real-world examples.

The book is organized for both quick reference and in-depth learning. You can use it to look up the syntax and usage of specific functions when you're in a hurry, or you can explore the examples and explanations to deepen your understanding of SQL functions.

In "SQL Functions Dictionary," you'll find answers to questions like:

How do I sum up values in a column efficiently?

What's the best way to calculate the average of a set of data?

How can I count the number of records that meet certain conditions?

What functions can help me find the minimum or maximum values in a dataset?

How do I manipulate and format date and time data effectively?

What are the most commonly used string functions for text manipulation?

How can I harness the power of mathematical and statistical functions?

Each function is accompanied by clear and concise examples, providing you with the practical knowledge needed to apply these functions to your unique data analysis challenges.

Whether you're seeking to improve your SQL skills or you're a seasoned SQL pro looking for quick reference materials, "SQL Functions Dictionary" is your trusted companion in the world of SQL. By unlocking the potential of SQL functions, you'll be better equipped to extract valuable insights, make informed decisions, and enhance your data analysis capabilities.

We invite you to delve into this invaluable resource and discover the power of SQL functions. Welcome to the world of SQL made simpler and more effective with "SQL Functions Dictionary."

Happy querying and exploring!

I.
Statistical functions

1.1 COUNT

Description:

The COUNT function in SQL is an aggregate function that calculates and returns the number of rows or records in a result set that meets a specified condition. It is commonly used to count the occurrences of values in a column or to count all rows in a table. COUNT is a versatile function that can be applied to different scenarios to provide essential insights into your data.

Syntax:

The basic syntax of the COUNT function is as follows:

```sql
COUNT(expression)
```

- `expression`: This can be an asterisk `*` to count all rows, a specific column name, or an expression that evaluates to a column or set of values you want to count.

Examples:

1. Count All Rows:

   To count all rows in a table, you can use the COUNT function with an asterisk. Here's an example with a table named `Students`:

```sql
SELECT COUNT(*) FROM Students;
```

Result: This query will return the total number of rows in the `Students` table.

2. Count Rows Meeting a Condition:

You can use COUNT to count the rows that meet a specific condition. In this example, we want to count the students who scored higher than 90 on an exam:

```sql
SELECT COUNT(*) FROM Students WHERE ExamScore > 90;
```

Result: This query will return the count of students who scored more than 90 in the `ExamScore` column.

Explanation of the Code:

- `SELECT COUNT(*)`: This part of the code selects the count of rows from the result set.

- `FROM Students`: It specifies the table (in this case, "Students") from which you want to count the rows.

- `WHERE ExamScore > 90`: This is an optional clause that filters the rows based on the specified condition. In the second example, it counts rows where the "ExamScore" is greater than 90.

Tips:

- COUNT is often used with GROUP BY to count rows within specific groups or categories.

- If you want to count the number of distinct values in a column, you can use COUNT(DISTINCT expression).

- Be cautious when using COUNT with text columns, as it counts non-null values, not distinct values.

- Always ensure that the condition in the WHERE clause accurately reflects the criteria for counting the desired rows.

1.2 SUM

Description:

The SUM function in SQL is an aggregate function used to calculate the sum or total of a set of numeric values within a specified column. It is widely employed for performing summation operations on data, particularly in scenarios where you need to obtain the total value of a specific numeric attribute.

Syntax:

The basic syntax of the SUM function is as follows:

```sql
SUM(expression)
```

- `expression`: This is the column or numeric expression that you want to sum.

Examples:

1. Sum All Values:

To calculate the sum of all values in a specific column, you can use the SUM function. For instance, with a table named `Sales` and a column `Revenue`:

```sql
SELECT SUM(Revenue) FROM Sales;
```

Result: This query will return the total sum of the values in the `Revenue` column.

2. Sum Values Based on a Condition:

You can use the SUM function to sum values that meet a certain condition. Here's an example where we want to find the total revenue for a specific product category, e.g., 'Electronics':

```sql
SELECT SUM(Revenue) FROM Sales WHERE Category = 'Electronics';
```

Result: This query will return the sum of the 'Revenue' values only for rows where the 'Category' is 'Electronics'.

Explanation of the Code:

- `SELECT SUM(Revenue)`: This part of the code selects the sum of values from the result set based on the expression provided.

- `FROM Sales`: It specifies the table (in this case, "Sales") from which you want to calculate the sum.

- `WHERE Category = 'Electronics'`: This is an optional clause that filters the rows based on the specified condition. In the second example, it calculates the sum of 'Revenue' only for rows with 'Category' equal to 'Electronics'.

Tips:

- SUM is an aggregate function, commonly used in combination with GROUP BY for summarizing data within specific groups.

- Ensure that the column specified in the SUM function contains numeric data, as it can't sum non-numeric or text data.

- Be cautious when dealing with NULL values, as the SUM function will ignore them.

- When using SUM with a condition, make sure the condition accurately reflects the criteria for summing the desired values.

1.3 AVG

Description:

The AVG function in SQL is an aggregate function used to calculate the average or mean of a set of numeric values within a specified column. It is widely utilized to find the typical value in a dataset, making it particularly useful for performing data analysis and reporting tasks.

Syntax:

The basic syntax of the AVG function is as follows:

```sql
AVG(expression)
```

- `expression`: This is the column or numeric expression that you want to find the average for.

Examples:

1. Find the Average of All Values:

To calculate the average of all values in a specific column, you can use the AVG function. For instance, with a table named `Sales` and a column `Price`:

```sql
SELECT AVG(Price) FROM Sales;
```

Result: This query will return the average (mean) of the values in the `Price` column.

2. Find the Average for a Specific Category:

You can use the AVG function to find the average for a subset of rows meeting a certain condition. Here's an example where we want to find the average price for products in the 'Electronics' category:

```sql
SELECT AVG(Price) FROM Sales WHERE Category = 'Electronics';
```

Result: This query will return the average price only for rows where the 'Category' is 'Electronics'.

Explanation of the Code:

- `SELECT AVG(Price)`: This part of the code selects the average (mean) of values from the result set based on the expression provided.

- `FROM Sales`: It specifies the table (in this case, "Sales") from which you want to calculate the average.

- `WHERE Category = 'Electronics'`: This is an optional clause that filters the rows based on the specified condition. In the second example, it calculates the average 'Price' only for rows with 'Category' equal to 'Electronics'.

Tips:

- AVG is an aggregate function, often used in combination with GROUP BY for summary data within specific groups.

- Ensure that the column specified in the AVG function contains numeric data, as it can't find the average of non-numeric or text data.

- Be aware of NULL values; AVG will ignore them when calculating the average.

- When using AVG with a condition, ensure that the condition accurately reflects the criteria for finding the average of the desired values.

1.4 MIN

Description:

The MIN function in SQL is an aggregate function used to find the minimum value in a specified column containing numeric or date values. It is frequently employed to identify the smallest value within a dataset, making it valuable for various analytical and reporting tasks.

Syntax:

The basic syntax of the MIN function is as follows:

```sql
MIN(expression)
```

- `expression`: This is the column or numeric expression from which you want to find the minimum value.

Examples:

1. Find the Minimum Value:

To identify the minimum value in a specific column, you can use the MIN function. For instance, with a table named `Inventory` and a column `UnitPrice`:

```sql
SELECT MIN(UnitPrice) FROM Inventory;
```

Result: This query will return the smallest value in the `UnitPrice` column.

2. Find the Minimum Date:

You can also use the MIN function to find the earliest date in a date column. Here's an example with a table named `Orders` and a column `OrderDate`:

```sql
SELECT MIN(OrderDate) FROM Orders;
```

Result: This query will return the earliest (minimum) date in the `OrderDate` column.

Explanation of the Code:

- `SELECT MIN(UnitPrice)`: This part of the code selects the minimum value from the result set based on the expression provided.

- `FROM Inventory`: It specifies the table (in this case, "Inventory") from which you want to find the minimum value.

- `SELECT MIN(OrderDate)`: In the second example, this part selects the earliest date in the `OrderDate` column from the "Orders" table.

Tips:

- MIN is an aggregate function and is often used with GROUP BY to identify the minimum values within specific groups or categories.

- Ensure that the column specified in the MIN function contains values of the appropriate data type, such as numeric or date values.

- Be cautious when dealing with NULL values; MIN will return NULL if there are NULL values in the column.

- When using MIN in combination with other columns, make sure the query accurately reflects the criteria for finding the minimum value in your dataset.

1.5 MAX

Description:

The MAX function in SQL is an aggregate function used to find the maximum value in a specified column containing numeric or date values. It is commonly used to identify the largest value within a dataset, making it valuable for various analytical and reporting tasks.

Syntax:

The basic syntax of the MAX function is as follows:

```sql
MAX(expression)
```

- `expression`: This is the column or numeric expression from which you want to find the maximum value.

Examples:

1. Find the Maximum Value:

To identify the maximum value in a specific column, you can use the MAX function. For instance, with a table named `Inventory` and a column `UnitPrice`:

```sql
SELECT MAX(UnitPrice) FROM Inventory;
```

Result: This query will return the largest value in the `UnitPrice` column.

2. Find the Maximum Date:

You can also use the MAX function to find the latest date in a date column. Here's an example with a table named `Orders` and a column `OrderDate`:

```sql
SELECT MAX(OrderDate) FROM Orders;
```

Result: This query will return the latest (maximum) date in the `OrderDate` column.

Explanation of the Code:

- `SELECT MAX(UnitPrice)`: This part of the code selects the maximum value from the result set based on the expression provided.

- `FROM Inventory`: It specifies the table (in this case, "Inventory") from which you want to find the maximum value.

- `SELECT MAX(OrderDate)`: In the second example, this part selects the latest date in the `OrderDate` column from the "Orders" table.

Tips:

- MAX is an aggregate function and is often used with GROUP BY to identify the maximum values within specific groups or categories.

- Ensure that the column specified in the MAX function contains values of the appropriate data type, such as numeric or date values.

- Be cautious when dealing with NULL values; MAX will return NULL if there are NULL values in the column.

- When using MAX in combination with other columns, make sure the query accurately reflects the criteria for finding the maximum value in your dataset.

1.6 STDDEV or STDEV

Description:

The STDDEV (Standard Deviation) function in SQL is an aggregate function used to calculate the standard deviation of a set of numeric values within a specified column. Standard deviation measures the amount of variation or dispersion in a dataset, making it a valuable tool for assessing the spread or consistency of data values. It is widely employed for statistical analysis, data quality assessment, and risk assessment.

Syntax:

The basic syntax of the STDDEV function is as follows:

```sql
STDDEV(expression)
```

- `expression`: This is the column or numeric expression from which you want to calculate the standard deviation.

Examples:

1. Calculate the Standard Deviation:

To find the standard deviation of a specific column, you can use the STDDEV function. For example, with a table named `Grades` and a column `Score`:

```sql
SELECT STDDEV(Score) FROM Grades;
```

Result: This query will return the standard deviation of the values in the `Score` column.

2. Calculate the Standard Deviation for a Specific Group:

You can use STDDEV in combination with GROUP BY to calculate standard deviation within specific groups or categories. Here's an example where you want to calculate the standard deviation of scores for different courses in the `Grades` table:

```sql
SELECT Course, STDDEV(Score) FROM Grades GROUP BY Course;
```

Result: This query will return the standard deviation of scores for each distinct course in the `Grades` table, grouped by the "Course" column.

Explanation of the Code:

- `SELECT STDDEV(Score)`: This part of the code selects the standard deviation of values from the result set based on the expression provided.

- `FROM Grades`: It specifies the table (in this case, "Grades") from which you want to calculate the standard deviation.

- `GROUP BY Course`: In the second example, this part groups the data by the "Course" column, and for each group, it calculates the standard deviation of scores.

Tips:

- STDDEV is an aggregate function and is particularly useful when you want to understand the spread of data or analyze data variations.

- Ensure that the column specified in the STDDEV function contains numeric data, as it can't calculate the standard deviation for non-numeric or text data.

- Be cautious when dealing with NULL values; STDDEV may ignore them or return NULL if there are NULL values in the column.

- Use STDDEV in combination with GROUP BY for group-level standard deviation calculations, which can be helpful for comparing variations across categories.

1.7 VARIANCE

Description:

The VARIANCE function in SQL is an aggregate function used to calculate the variance of a set of numeric values within a specified column. Variance measures the spread or dispersion of data points from the mean or average, making it a valuable tool for analyzing data variations and data quality assessment. It is particularly useful in statistical analysis and hypothesis testing.

Syntax:

The basic syntax of the VARIANCE function is as follows:

```sql
VARIANCE(expression)
```

- `expression`: This is the column or numeric expression from which you want to calculate the variance.

Examples:

1. Calculate the Variance:

To find the variance of a specific column, you can use the VARIANCE function. For example, with a table named `Sales` and a column `Revenue`:

```sql
SELECT VARIANCE(Revenue) FROM Sales;
```

Result: This query will return the variance of the values in the `Revenue` column.

2. Calculate the Variance for a Specific Group:

You can use VARIANCE in combination with GROUP BY to calculate variance within specific groups or categories. Here's an example where you want to calculate the variance of revenue for different product categories in the `Sales` table:

```sql
SELECT Category, VARIANCE(Revenue) FROM Sales GROUP BY Category;
```

Result: This query will return the variance of revenue for each distinct product category in the `Sales` table, grouped by the "Category" column.

Explanation of the Code:

- `SELECT VARIANCE(Revenue)`: This part of the code selects the variance of values from the result set based on the expression provided.

- `FROM Sales`: It specifies the table (in this case, "Sales") from which you want to calculate the variance.

- `GROUP BY Category`: In the second example, this part groups the data by the "Category" column, and for each group, it calculates the variance of revenue.

Tips:

- VARIANCE is an aggregate function and is particularly useful when you want to understand the spread of data or assess data variations.

- Ensure that the column specified in the VARIANCE function contains numeric data, as it can't calculate the variance for non-numeric or text data.

- Be cautious when dealing with NULL values; VARIANCE may ignore them or return NULL if there are NULL values in the column.

- Use VARIANCE in combination with GROUP BY for group-level variance calculations, which can be helpful for comparing variations across categories or groups.

1.8 MEDIAN

Description:

The MEDIAN function in SQL is used to calculate the median of a set of numeric values within a specified column. The median is the middle value in a dataset when it is sorted in ascending order. It is a valuable measure of central tendency, especially when dealing with data that may contain outliers or extreme values. MEDIAN is useful for statistical analysis, data distribution assessment, and understanding data patterns.

Syntax:

The basic syntax of the MEDIAN function is as follows:

```sql
MEDIAN(expression)
```

- `expression`: This is the column or numeric expression from which you want to calculate the median.

Examples:

1. Calculate the Median:

To find the median of a specific column, you can use the MEDIAN function. For instance, with a table named `Salary` and a column `MonthlyIncome`:

```sql
SELECT MEDIAN(MonthlyIncome) FROM Salary;
```

Result: This query will return the median value of the `MonthlyIncome` values.

2. Calculate the Median for a Specific Group:

You can use MEDIAN in combination with GROUP BY to calculate the median within specific groups or categories. Here's an example where you want to calculate the median income for different job positions in the `Salary` table:

```sql
SELECT JobPosition, MEDIAN(MonthlyIncome) FROM Salary GROUP BY JobPosition;
```

Result: This query will return the median income for each distinct job position in the `Salary` table, grouped by the "JobPosition" column.

Explanation of the Code:

- `SELECT MEDIAN(MonthlyIncome)`: This part of the code selects the median value from the result set based on the expression provided.

- `FROM Salary`: It specifies the table (in this case, "Salary") from which you want to calculate the median.

- `GROUP BY JobPosition`: In the second example, this part groups the data by the "JobPosition" column, and for each group, it calculates the median of MonthlyIncome.

Tips:

- MEDIAN is a valuable measure when analyzing data with skewed distributions or potential outliers, as it is not affected by extreme values.

- Ensure that the column specified in the MEDIAN function contains numeric data, as it cannot calculate the median for non-numeric or text data.

- Be cautious when dealing with NULL values; MEDIAN may ignore them or return NULL if there are NULL values in the column.

- Use MEDIAN in combination with GROUP BY for group-level median calculations, which can be useful for comparing central values across categories or groups.

1.9 MODE

Description:

The MODE function in SQL, also known as the statistical mode, is used to find the most frequently occurring value within a set of data in a specified column. The mode represents the value that appears with the highest frequency and is used to identify the central tendency or the most typical value in a dataset. MODE is valuable for data distribution analysis, especially when you want to find the most common category or value.

Syntax:

The basic syntax of the MODE function can vary depending on the database system you are using. It is not a standard SQL function, and some database systems do not directly support it. However, you can typically find the mode using subqueries or other workarounds, as shown in the examples below.

Examples:

1. Calculate the Mode (using a subquery):

To find the mode of a specific column, you can use a subquery. For instance, with a table named `Colors` and a column `Color`:

```sql
SELECT Color
FROM Colors
GROUP BY Color
HAVING COUNT(Color) = (
    SELECT MAX(Count) FROM (
        SELECT Color, COUNT(Color) AS Count
```

```
    FROM Colors
    GROUP BY Color
  ) AS CountTable
);
```

Result: This query will return the mode value(s) in the `Color` column. It groups the data by color, counts the occurrences of each color, and selects the one(s) with the highest count.

2. Calculate the Mode for a Specific Group:

You can use similar subqueries to calculate the mode within specific groups or categories. Here's an example where you want to find the mode color for different products in the `Products` table:

```sql
SELECT ProductType, Color
FROM Products
GROUP BY ProductType, Color
HAVING COUNT(Color) = (
  SELECT MAX(Count) FROM (
    SELECT ProductType, Color, COUNT(Color) AS Count
    FROM Products
    GROUP BY ProductType, Color
  ) AS CountTable
);
```

Result: This query will return the mode color for each distinct product type in the `Products` table, grouped by "ProductType."

Explanation of the Code:

- These queries use subqueries to find the most frequently occurring value(s) within the dataset.

- The subqueries first group the data by the column(s) of interest (e.g., "Color" or "ProductType").

- They then count the occurrences of each value within the group.

- The outer query selects the value(s) with the highest count, which represents the mode.

Tips:

- The availability of the MODE function and the specific syntax can vary between database systems. If your database system supports a native MODE function, it's advisable to use it.

- When using subqueries to find the mode, ensure that the subqueries are efficient, especially when dealing with large datasets.

- Be cautious when dealing with multimodal datasets (datasets with multiple modes), as the queries provided will return only one mode, even if there are multiple values with the same highest frequency.

- Be aware of NULL values; you may need to handle them appropriately to get accurate mode results.

1.10 CORR

Description:

The CORR function in SQL is used to calculate the Pearson correlation coefficient between two sets of numeric values. The Pearson correlation coefficient, also known as Pearson's r, measures the linear relationship between two variables. It is a valuable tool for assessing the strength and direction of the relationship between two sets of data. A positive correlation indicates a positive linear relationship, while a negative correlation indicates a negative linear relationship.

Syntax:

The basic syntax of the CORR function is as follows:

```sql
CORR(expression1, expression2)
```

- `expression1` and `expression2`: These are the two numeric columns or expressions for which you want to calculate the correlation coefficient.

Examples:

1. Calculate the Correlation Coefficient:

To calculate the correlation between two columns, you can use the CORR function. For instance, with a table named `Sales` and columns `Price` and `SalesQuantity`:

```sql
SELECT CORR(Price, SalesQuantity) FROM Sales;
```

Result: This query will return the Pearson correlation coefficient between the `Price` and `SalesQuantity` columns. The coefficient will indicate the direction and strength of the linear relationship.

Explanation of the Code:

- `SELECT CORR(Price, SalesQuantity)`: This part of the code calculates the Pearson correlation coefficient between the `Price` and `SalesQuantity` columns in the result set.

Tips:

- The Pearson correlation coefficient ranges from -1 to 1. A value of 1 indicates a perfect positive linear relationship, -1 indicates a perfect negative linear relationship, and 0 indicates no linear relationship.

- Be sure to use this function with two numeric columns or expressions, as it calculates the correlation between numerical data.

- The correlation coefficient is a measure of linear association and may not capture non-linear relationships.

- Always consider the context and domain knowledge when interpreting correlation coefficients; correlation does not imply causation.

1.11 COVAR_POP

Description:

The COVAR_POP function in SQL is used to calculate the population covariance between two sets of numeric values. Covariance measures the degree to which two variables change together. In the context of COVAR_POP, it provides a measure of how two variables deviate from their respective means in the same direction. A positive covariance indicates that both variables tend to increase together, while a negative covariance suggests that one tends to decrease when the other increases.

Syntax:

The basic syntax of the COVAR_POP function is as follows:

```sql
COVAR_POP(expression1, expression2)
```

- `expression1` and `expression2`: These are the two numeric columns or expressions for which you want to calculate the population covariance.

Examples:

1. Calculate the Population Covariance:

To calculate the population covariance between two columns, you can use the COVAR_POP function. For instance, with a table named `Stocks` and columns `Price` and `Volume`:

```sql
SELECT COVAR_POP(Price, Volume) FROM Stocks;
```

Result: This query will return the population covariance between the `Price` and `Volume` columns. The covariance value indicates how these two variables change together within the entire population.

Explanation of the Code:

- `SELECT COVAR_POP(Price, Volume)`: This part of the code calculates the population covariance between the `Price` and `Volume` columns in the result set.

Tips:

- The population covariance is a measure of the extent to which two variables move together in the entire dataset. A positive value suggests a positive relationship, while a negative value suggests a negative relationship.

- Be sure to use this function with two numeric columns or expressions, as it calculates the covariance between numerical data.

- Covariance can be influenced by the scale of the variables, making it challenging to compare covariances between different datasets. To address this, some statisticians use the correlation coefficient to normalize the covariance.

- Be cautious when interpreting covariance results, as it may not be as intuitive as the correlation coefficient for measuring the strength and direction of a linear relationship.

1.12 COVAR_SAMP

Description:

The COVAR_SAMP function in SQL is used to calculate the sample covariance between two sets of numeric values. Covariance measures the degree to which two variables change together. In the context of COVAR_SAMP, it provides a measure of how two variables deviate from their respective means in the same direction within a sample dataset. Sample covariance is used to estimate the population covariance based on a sample of data.

Syntax:

The basic syntax of the COVAR_SAMP function is as follows:

```sql
COVAR_SAMP(expression1, expression2)
```

- `expression1` and `expression2`: These are the two numeric columns or expressions for which you want to calculate the sample covariance.

Examples:

1. Calculate the Sample Covariance:

To calculate the sample covariance between two columns, you can use the COVAR_SAMP function. For instance, with a table named `Returns` and columns `Stock1Returns` and `Stock2Returns`:

```sql
SELECT COVAR_SAMP(Stock1Returns, Stock2Returns) FROM Returns;
```

Result: This query will return the sample covariance between the `Stock1Returns` and `Stock2Returns` columns. The covariance value indicates how these two variables change together within the sample dataset.

Explanation of the Code:

- `SELECT COVAR_SAMP(Stock1Returns, Stock2Returns)`: This part of the code calculates the sample covariance between the `Stock1Returns` and `Stock2Returns` columns in the result set.

Tips:

- Sample covariance measures the extent to which two variables move together within a sample dataset. It is often used when you have a sample of data and want to estimate the covariance between variables in the entire population.

- Be sure to use this function with two numeric columns or expressions, as it calculates the covariance between numerical data.

- Covariance can be influenced by the scale of the variables, making it challenging to compare covariances between different datasets. To address this, some statisticians use the correlation coefficient to normalize the covariance.

- When interpreting sample covariance results, keep in mind that it is an estimate of the population covariance, and the sample size can affect the reliability of the estimate. c

1.13 PERCENTILE_CONT

Description:

The PERCENTILE_CONT function in SQL is used to calculate the specific percentile value of a numeric column within a given dataset. Percentiles represent the value below which a given percentage of the data falls. For example, the 50th percentile is the median, and it divides the data into two equal parts. PERCENTILE_CONT is valuable for analyzing data distribution and identifying values at specific positions within a dataset.

Syntax:

The basic syntax of the PERCENTILE_CONT function is as follows:

```sql
PERCENTILE_CONT(percent) WITHIN GROUP (ORDER BY expression)
```

- `percent`: This is the percentile value you want to calculate, typically expressed as a decimal (e.g., 0.5 for the median).

- `expression`: This is the numeric column or expression from which you want to calculate the percentile.

Examples:

1. Calculate the Median (50th Percentile):

To calculate the median of a specific column, you can use the PERCENTILE_CONT function. For example, with a table named `Scores` and a column `Score`:

```sql
SELECT PERCENTILE_CONT(0.5) WITHIN GROUP (ORDER BY Score) FROM Scores;
```

```
```

Result: This query will return the median (50th percentile) of the `Score` column. The `ORDER BY` clause ensures the data is sorted by the `Score` column to find the midpoint.

Explanation of the Code:

- `SELECT PERCENTILE_CONT(0.5) WITHIN GROUP (ORDER BY Score)`: This part of the code calculates the median (50th percentile) of the `Score` column. The `ORDER BY Score` clause ensures that the data is sorted by the `Score` column before finding the midpoint.

Tips:

- The `percent` parameter should be a decimal value between 0 and 1, where 0 represents the minimum value, 1 represents the maximum value, and 0.5 represents the median.

- The `expression` should be a numeric column, and the `ORDER BY` clause specifies the sorting order for the calculation.

- PERCENTILE_CONT is particularly useful for analyzing the distribution of data and identifying values that divide the data at specific percentiles.

- Be aware that there are other similar functions like PERCENTILE_DISC, which provides discrete values from the dataset rather than interpolated values. The choice depends on your specific use case.

1.14 PERCENTILE_DISC

Description:

The PERCENTILE_DISC function in SQL is used to calculate a specific percentile value of a numeric column within a given dataset. Unlike PERCENTILE_CONT, which returns interpolated values, PERCENTILE_DISC returns actual discrete values from the dataset. Percentiles represent the value below which a given percentage of the data falls. PERCENTILE_DISC is valuable for identifying specific values at particular percentiles within a dataset.

Syntax:

The basic syntax of the PERCENTILE_DISC function is as follows:

```sql
PERCENTILE_DISC(percent) WITHIN GROUP (ORDER BY expression)
```

- `percent`: This is the percentile value you want to calculate, typically expressed as a decimal (e.g., 0.5 for the median).

- `expression`: This is the numeric column or expression from which you want to calculate the percentile.

Examples:

1. Calculate the Median (50th Percentile):

To calculate the median of a specific column, you can use the PERCENTILE_DISC function. For example, with a table named `Scores` and a column `Score`:

```sql
SELECT PERCENTILE_DISC(0.5) WITHIN GROUP (ORDER BY Score) FROM Scores;
```

```

Result: This query will return the median (50th percentile) of the `Score` column. The `ORDER BY` clause ensures the data is sorted by the `Score` column to find the midpoint.

**Explanation of the Code:**

- `SELECT PERCENTILE_DISC(0.5) WITHIN GROUP (ORDER BY Score)`: This part of the code calculates the median (50th percentile) of the `Score` column. The `ORDER BY Score` clause ensures that the data is sorted by the `Score` column before finding the midpoint.

**Tips:**

- The `percent` parameter should be a decimal value between 0 and 1, where 0 represents the minimum value, 1 represents the maximum value, and 0.5 represents the median.

- The `expression` should be a numeric column, and the `ORDER BY` clause specifies the sorting order for the calculation.

- PERCENTILE_DISC is particularly useful when you want to identify specific values in the dataset at particular percentiles, especially for tasks such as defining score cutoffs or identifying thresholds.

- Be aware that there are other similar functions like PERCENTILE_CONT, which provides interpolated values between dataset values rather than discrete values. The choice depends on your specific use case.
```

1.15 RANK

Description:

The RANK function in SQL is used to assign a rank to each row within a result set based on the values in one or more columns. Ranks are assigned in ascending order, with the lowest value getting a rank of 1. In the case of tied values, the RANK function assigns the same rank to all tied rows and leaves gaps in the ranking sequence. RANK is often used to identify the relative position of rows in a dataset.

Syntax:

The basic syntax of the RANK function is as follows:

```sql
RANK() OVER (PARTITION BY partition_expression ORDER BY sort_expression)
```

- `partition_expression`: An optional clause that divides the result set into partitions to rank rows within each partition. If not specified, the entire result set is treated as one partition.

- `sort_expression`: The column or columns by which the rows are sorted to assign ranks. Rows are ranked in ascending order based on this expression.

Examples:

1. Assign Ranks to Students Based on Their Scores:

To assign ranks to students in a table named `Students` based on their scores:

```sql
SELECT StudentName, Score, RANK() OVER (ORDER BY Score DESC) AS Rank
FROM Students;
```

Result: This query assigns ranks to students in descending order of their scores, with the top scorer receiving a rank of 1.

Explanation of the Code:

- `SELECT StudentName, Score, RANK() OVER (ORDER BY Score DESC) AS Rank`: This part of the code selects the student's name, score, and assigns a rank to each student based on their score. The `ORDER BY Score DESC` clause sorts the rows by score in descending order.

Tips:

- The RANK function is often used in combination with the `OVER` clause to provide the ranking context.

- Be cautious when using the `PARTITION BY` clause, as it divides the result set into partitions for ranking. This can be useful when you want to rank rows within specific groups.

- In cases of tied values, the RANK function assigns the same rank to all tied rows and leaves gaps in the ranking sequence. If you want to avoid gaps, you can use the DENSE_RANK function, which assigns consecutive ranks to tied values.

- Pay attention to the sorting order (ASC or DESC) when using the `ORDER BY` clause, as it determines whether higher or lower values receive higher ranks.

1.16 NTILE

Description:

The NTILE function in SQL is used to divide the result set into a specified number of approximately equal parts, assigning a group number to each row based on its rank within the ordered result set. NTILE is often used to distribute data evenly into percentile groups or quartiles. It helps in analyzing data distribution and understanding the relative position of rows within the result set.

Syntax:

The basic syntax of the NTILE function is as follows:

```sql
NTILE(number_of_groups) OVER (ORDER BY sort_expression)
```

- `number_of_groups`: The integer value that specifies the number of groups into which the result set will be divided.

- `sort_expression`: The column or columns by which the rows are sorted for division into groups.

Examples:

1. Divide Students into Quartiles:

To divide a list of students from a table named `Students` into quartiles based on their scores:

```sql
SELECT StudentName, Score, NTILE(4) OVER (ORDER BY Score) AS Quartile
FROM Students;
```

Result: This query assigns quartiles to students based on their scores, with Quartile 1 containing the lowest-scoring students and Quartile 4 containing the highest-scoring students.

Explanation of the Code:

- `SELECT StudentName, Score, NTILE(4) OVER (ORDER BY Score) AS Quartile`: This part of the code selects the student's name, score, and assigns a quartile to each student based on their score. The `ORDER BY Score` clause sorts the rows by score.

Tips:

- The `number_of_groups` parameter in NTILE specifies how many groups you want to divide the result set into. For quartiles, use 4; for percentiles, use 100, and so on.

- NTILE is particularly useful when you want to distribute data evenly into groups based on rank or position.

- Ensure that the `ORDER BY` clause specifies the sorting order (ASC or DESC) based on your requirement. The sorting determines the ranks and, consequently, the group assignments.

- Be aware that NTILE may not result in perfectly equal-sized groups, especially when the number of rows is not evenly divisible by the specified number of groups. It distributes rows as evenly as possible.

II.
Date and time functions

2.1 CURRENT_DATE

Description:

The CURRENT_DATE function in SQL is used to retrieve the current date from the database system or server. It returns the current date without the time component, making it useful for tasks that involve date-related comparisons and calculations. CURRENT_DATE is often used in SQL queries to filter or manipulate data based on the current date.

Syntax:

The syntax for the CURRENT_DATE function is straightforward. You simply call it as follows:

```sql
CURRENT_DATE
```

Examples:

1. Retrieve the Current Date:

To retrieve the current date, you can use the CURRENT_DATE function in a SQL query:

```sql
SELECT CURRENT_DATE;
```

```

Result: This query will return the current date, such as '2023-10-12'.

**Explanation of the Code:**

- `SELECT CURRENT_DATE`: This part of the code simply retrieves the current date without any additional parameters.

**Tips:**

- CURRENT_DATE is typically used for tasks that involve date-based filtering or calculations within SQL queries.

- Be aware of the date format used by your database system; it can vary, so it's important to understand the specific format in use.

- CURRENT_DATE is often combined with other date-related functions to perform more complex operations, such as calculating the age of individuals or finding records with dates within a specific range.

- Ensure that the database system or server is set to the correct date and time zone, as the output of CURRENT_DATE depends on the system's settings.
```

2.2 CURRENT_TIME

Description:

The CURRENT_TIME function in SQL is used to retrieve the current time from the database system or server. It returns the current time, including hours, minutes, seconds, and fractions of a second. CURRENT_TIME is often used in SQL queries to record the exact time of an event, time-based filtering, or other time-related operations.

Syntax:

The syntax for the CURRENT_TIME function is simple. You call it as follows:

```sql
CURRENT_TIME
```

Examples:

1. Retrieve the Current Time:

To retrieve the current time, you can use the CURRENT_TIME function in a SQL query:

```sql
SELECT CURRENT_TIME;
```

Result: This query will return the current time, such as '15:30:45.123456'.

Explanation of the Code:

- `SELECT CURRENT_TIME`: This part of the code simply retrieves the current time without any additional parameters.

Tips:

- CURRENT_TIME is typically used for tasks that require recording the current time or time-based filtering within SQL queries.

- Be aware of the time format used by your database system; it can vary, so it's important to understand the specific format in use, including whether fractions of a second are included.

- CURRENT_TIME is often combined with other date and time-related functions to perform more complex operations, such as recording timestamps for data entries or calculating time intervals.

- Ensure that the database system or server is set to the correct time zone, as the output of CURRENT_TIME depends on the system's settings.

2.3 CURRENT_TIMESTAMP

Description:

The CURRENT_TIMESTAMP function in SQL is used to retrieve the current date and time from the database system or server. It returns the current date and time, including the year, month, day, hours, minutes, seconds, and fractions of a second. CURRENT_TIMESTAMP is often used in SQL queries to record the exact timestamp of an event, time-based filtering, or other time-related operations.

Syntax:

The syntax for the CURRENT_TIMESTAMP function is straightforward. You call it as follows:

```sql
CURRENT_TIMESTAMP
```

Examples:

1. Retrieve the Current Timestamp:

To retrieve the current timestamp, you can use the CURRENT_TIMESTAMP function in a SQL query:

```sql
SELECT CURRENT_TIMESTAMP;
```

Result: This query will return the current timestamp, such as '2023-10-12 15:30:45.123456'.

Explanation of the Code:

- `SELECT CURRENT_TIMESTAMP`: This part of the code simply retrieves the current timestamp without any additional parameters.

Tips:

- CURRENT_TIMESTAMP is typically used for tasks that require recording the exact timestamp of an event, including both date and time, or time-based filtering within SQL queries.

- Be aware of the timestamp format used by your database system; it can vary, so it's important to understand the specific format in use, including whether fractions of a second are included.

- CURRENT_TIMESTAMP is often combined with other date and time-related functions to perform more complex operations, such as recording timestamps for data entries or calculating time intervals.

- Ensure that the database system or server is set to the correct time zone, as the output of CURRENT_TIMESTAMP depends on the system's settings.

2.4 DATEADD

Description:

The DATEADD function in SQL is used to add or subtract a specified number of date or time intervals to a given date or time value. This function is commonly used for performing date and time calculations, such as adding days to a date, subtracting hours from a timestamp, or other similar operations.

Syntax:

The syntax for the DATEADD function is as follows:

```sql
DATEADD(interval, number, date)
```

- `interval`: The interval of time to add or subtract, such as 'day,' 'hour,' 'minute,' 'month,' 'year,' etc.

- `number`: The number of intervals to add or subtract. This can be a positive or negative integer.

- `date`: The starting date or time to which you want to add or subtract the intervals.

Examples:

1. Add 7 Days to a Date:

To add 7 days to a specific date, you can use the DATEADD function. For instance, to add 7 days to a date '2023-10-12':

```sql
SELECT DATEADD(day, 7, '2023-10-12') AS NewDate;
```

```

Result: This query will return the new date '2023-10-19' after adding 7 days to '2023-10-12'.

**Explanation of the Code:**

- `SELECT DATEADD(day, 7, '2023-10-12') AS NewDate`: This part of the code adds 7 days to the date '2023-10-12' and stores the result in the 'NewDate' column.

**Tips:**

- The `interval` parameter specifies the unit of time you want to add or subtract. Common intervals include 'day,' 'hour,' 'minute,' 'month,' 'year,' etc.

- The `number` parameter determines how many intervals to add or subtract. It can be a positive or negative integer.

- The DATEADD function is useful for performing various date and time calculations in SQL, such as calculating future or past dates, adjusting timestamps, and more.

- Be cautious about the date format used in your SQL database system, as it can affect the interpretation of the input and output date values.
```

2.5 DATEDIFF

Description:

The DATEDIFF function in SQL is used to calculate the difference between two dates or times, expressed in terms of a specified time interval. It returns an integer value representing the number of units (e.g., days, months, years) that separate two date or time values. DATEDIFF is often used for calculating age, time intervals, or other date-based metrics.

Syntax:

The syntax for the DATEDIFF function is as follows:

```sql
DATEDIFF(interval, start_date, end_date)
```

- `interval`: The time interval for which you want to calculate the difference, such as 'day,' 'month,' 'year,' etc.

- `start_date`: The starting date or time.

- `end_date`: The ending date or time.

Examples:

1. Calculate the Number of Days Between Two Dates:

To calculate the number of days between two dates, you can use the DATEDIFF function. For instance, to calculate the number of days between '2023-10-12' and '2023-10-19':

```sql
SELECT DATEDIFF(day, '2023-10-12', '2023-10-19') AS DayDifference;
```

```
```

Result: This query will return '7' as the number of days between '2023-10-12' and '2023-10-19'.

Explanation of the Code:

- `SELECT DATEDIFF(day, '2023-10-12', '2023-10-19') AS DayDifference`: This part of the code calculates the difference in days between the two provided dates and stores the result in the 'DayDifference' column.

Tips:

- The `interval` parameter specifies the unit of time for which you want to calculate the difference. Common intervals include 'day,' 'month,' 'year,' etc.

- The DATEDIFF function is useful for various date-based calculations, such as calculating age, duration between events, or the time between two timestamps.

- Ensure that the date format used in your SQL database system is consistent with the input date values to obtain accurate results.

- Be mindful of how different database systems handle leap years, daylight saving time, and time zones, as these factors can affect the results when dealing with date and time differences.

2.6 DATEPART

Description:

The DATEPART function in SQL is used to extract a specific part or component of a date or time, such as the year, month, day, hour, minute, second, and more. It allows you to retrieve individual components from a date or time value, which can be useful for various date-related calculations and data extraction.

Syntax:

The syntax for the DATEPART function is as follows:

```sql
DATEPART(part, date)
```

- `part`: The specific part or component you want to extract from the date or time value, such as 'year,' 'month,' 'day,' 'hour,' 'minute,' 'second,' etc.

- `date`: The date or time value from which you want to extract the specified part.

Examples:

1. Extract the Year from a Date:

To extract the year from a date, you can use the DATEPART function. For instance, to extract the year from '2023-10-12':

```sql
SELECT DATEPART(year, '2023-10-12') AS YearPart;
```

Result: This query will return '2023' as the extracted year from '2023-10-12'.

Explanation of the Code:

- `SELECT DATEPART(year, '2023-10-12') AS YearPart`: This part of the code extracts the year component from the provided date and stores it in the 'YearPart' column.

Tips:

- The `part` parameter specifies the specific component you want to extract, and it should be a recognized date or time part (e.g., 'year,' 'month,' 'day,' 'hour,' 'minute,' 'second').

- DATEPART is useful for various date-related operations, such as extracting individual components for calculations, data filtering, or generating reports.

- Be aware of the date and time format used by your database system, as it can impact the interpretation of the input date values and the results of DATEPART.

- Always ensure that the data type of the column you are extracting from is a date or time type, as DATEPART requires a valid date or time value as input.

2.7 DAY

Description:

The DAY function in SQL is used to extract the day component from a date or datetime value. It returns the day of the month as an integer. DAY is commonly used to retrieve the day portion of a date for various date-related operations and data extraction.

Syntax:

The syntax for the DAY function is simple. You call it as follows:

```sql
DAY(date)
```

- `date`: The date or datetime value from which you want to extract the day component.

Examples:

1. Extract the Day from a Date:

To extract the day from a date, you can use the DAY function. For instance, to extract the day from '2023-10-12':

```sql
SELECT DAY('2023-10-12') AS DayOfMonth;
```

Result: This query will return '12' as the extracted day from '2023-10-12'.

Explanation of the Code:

- `SELECT DAY('2023-10-12') AS DayOfMonth`: This part of the code extracts the day component from the provided date and stores it in the 'DayOfMonth' column.

Tips:

- The DAY function is particularly useful when you need to retrieve the day part of a date for tasks like date filtering, generating monthly reports, or performing calculations based on day values.

- Ensure that the data type of the column you are using with DAY is a date or datetime type, as DAY expects a valid date or datetime value as input.

- Be aware of the date format used by your database system, as it can affect the interpretation of the input date values and the results provided by DAY.

- DAY returns an integer value representing the day of the month, which can range from 1 to 31. Be sure to consider the day's numeric representation in your SQL operations.

2.8 MONTH

Description:

The MONTH function in SQL is used to extract the month component from a date or datetime value. It returns the month as an integer, with values ranging from 1 (January) to 12 (December). MONTH is commonly used for tasks that require retrieving the month portion of a date for various date-related operations and data extraction.

Syntax:

The syntax for the MONTH function is straightforward. You call it as follows:

```sql
MONTH(date)
```

- `date`: The date or datetime value from which you want to extract the month component.

Examples:

1. Extract the Month from a Date:

To extract the month from a date, you can use the MONTH function. For instance, to extract the month from '2023-10-12':

```sql
SELECT MONTH('2023-10-12') AS MonthNumber;
```

Result: This query will return '10' as the extracted month from '2023-10-12'.

Explanation of the Code:

- `SELECT MONTH('2023-10-12') AS MonthNumber`: This part of the code extracts the month component from the provided date and stores it in the 'MonthNumber' column.

Tips:

- The MONTH function is particularly useful when you need to retrieve the month part of a date for tasks like monthly reporting, filtering data by month, or performing calculations based on month values.

- Ensure that the data type of the column you are using with MONTH is a date or datetime type, as MONTH expects a valid date or datetime value as input.

- Be aware of the date format used by your database system, as it can affect the interpretation of the input date values and the results provided by MONTH.

- MONTH returns an integer value representing the month, with values ranging from 1 to 12, corresponding to the months of the year. Be sure to consider this numeric representation in your SQL operations.

2.9 YEAR

Description:

The YEAR function in SQL is used to extract the year component from a date or datetime value. It returns the year as a four-digit integer. YEAR is commonly used for tasks that require retrieving the year portion of a date for various date-related operations and data extraction.

Syntax:

The syntax for the YEAR function is simple. You call it as follows:

```sql
YEAR(date)
```

- `date`: The date or datetime value from which you want to extract the year component.

Examples:

1. Extract the Year from a Date:

To extract the year from a date, you can use the YEAR function. For instance, to extract the year from '2023-10-12':

```sql
SELECT YEAR('2023-10-12') AS YearValue;
```

Result: This query will return '2023' as the extracted year from '2023-10-12'.

Explanation of the Code:

- `SELECT YEAR('2023-10-12') AS YearValue`: This part of the code extracts the year component from the provided date and stores it in the 'YearValue' column.

Tips:

- The YEAR function is particularly useful when you need to retrieve the year part of a date for tasks like yearly reporting, data filtering by year, or performing calculations based on year values.

- Ensure that the data type of the column you are using with YEAR is a date or datetime type, as YEAR expects a valid date or datetime value as input.

- Be aware of the date format used by your database system, as it can affect the interpretation of the input date values and the results provided by YEAR.

- YEAR returns a four-digit integer value representing the year. Be sure to consider this numeric representation in your SQL operations.

2.10 HOUR

Description:

The HOUR function in SQL is used to extract the hour component from a time or datetime value. It returns the hour as an integer, typically ranging from 0 to 23 in a 24-hour clock format. HOUR is commonly used for tasks that require retrieving the hour portion of a time for various time-related operations and data extraction.

Syntax:

The syntax for the HOUR function is as follows:

```sql
HOUR(time)
```

- `time`: The time or datetime value from which you want to extract the hour component.

Examples:

1. Extract the Hour from a Time:

To extract the hour from a time, you can use the HOUR function. For instance, to extract the hour from '15:30:45':

```sql
SELECT HOUR('15:30:45') AS HourValue;
```

Result: This query will return '15' as the extracted hour from '15:30:45'.

Explanation of the Code:

- `SELECT HOUR('15:30:45') AS HourValue`: This part of the code extracts the hour component from the provided time and stores it in the 'HourValue' column.

Tips:

- The HOUR function is particularly useful when you need to retrieve the hour part of a time for tasks like time-based reporting, filtering data by hour, or performing calculations based on hour values.

- Ensure that the data type of the column you are using with HOUR is a time or datetime type, as HOUR expects a valid time or datetime value as input.

- Be aware of the time format used by your database system, as it can affect the interpretation of the input time values and the results provided by HOUR.

- HOUR returns an integer value representing the hour, typically ranging from 0 to 23 in a 24-hour clock format. Be sure to consider this numeric representation in your SQL operations.

2.11 MINUTE

Description:

The MINUTE function in SQL is used to extract the minute component from a time or datetime value. It returns the minute as an integer, typically ranging from 0 to 59. MINUTE is commonly used for tasks that require retrieving the minute portion of a time for various time-related operations and data extraction.

Syntax:

The syntax for the MINUTE function is as follows:

```sql
MINUTE(time)
```

- `time`: The time or datetime value from which you want to extract the minute component.

Examples:

1. Extract the Minute from a Time:

To extract the minute from a time, you can use the MINUTE function. For instance, to extract the minute from '15:30:45':

```sql
SELECT MINUTE('15:30:45') AS MinuteValue;
```

Result: This query will return '30' as the extracted minute from '15:30:45'.

Explanation of the Code:

- `SELECT MINUTE('15:30:45') AS MinuteValue`: This part of the code extracts the minute component from the provided time and stores it in the 'MinuteValue' column.

Tips:

- The MINUTE function is particularly useful when you need to retrieve the minute part of a time for tasks like time-based reporting, filtering data by minute, or performing calculations based on minute values.

- Ensure that the data type of the column you are using with MINUTE is a time or datetime type, as MINUTE expects a valid time or datetime value as input.

- Be aware of the time format used by your database system, as it can affect the interpretation of the input time values and the results provided by MINUTE.

- MINUTE returns an integer value representing the minute, typically ranging from 0 to 59. Be sure to consider this numeric representation in your SQL operations.

2.12 SECOND

Description:

The SECOND function in SQL is used to extract the second component from a time or datetime value. It returns the second as an integer, typically ranging from 0 to 59. SECOND is commonly used for tasks that require retrieving the second portion of a time for various time-related operations and data extraction.

Syntax:

The syntax for the SECOND function is as follows:

```sql
SECOND(time)
```

- `time`: The time or datetime value from which you want to extract the second component.

Examples:

1. Extract the Second from a Time:

To extract the second from a time, you can use the SECOND function. For instance, to extract the second from '15:30:45':

```sql
SELECT SECOND('15:30:45') AS SecondValue;
```

Result: This query will return '45' as the extracted second from '15:30:45'.

Explanation of the Code:

- `SELECT SECOND('15:30:45') AS SecondValue`: This part of the code extracts the second component from the provided time and stores it in the 'SecondValue' column.

Tips:

- The SECOND function is particularly useful when you need to retrieve the second part of a time for tasks like time-based reporting, filtering data by second, or performing calculations based on second values.

- Ensure that the data type of the column you are using with SECOND is a time or datetime type, as SECOND expects a valid time or datetime value as input.

- Be aware of the time format used by your database system, as it can affect the interpretation of the input time values and the results provided by SECOND.

- SECOND returns an integer value representing the second, typically ranging from 0 to 59. Be sure to consider this numeric representation in your SQL operations.

2.13 NOW

Description:

The NOW function in SQL is used to retrieve the current date and time from the database system. It returns the current date and time as a datetime or timestamp value. NOW is commonly used for tasks that require capturing the current timestamp for various purposes such as recording when data was added or updated.

Syntax:

The syntax for the NOW function is simple. You call it as follows:

```sql
NOW()
```

Examples:

1. Retrieve the Current Date and Time:

To retrieve the current date and time, you can use the NOW function. For instance, to capture the current timestamp when a record is added to a table:

```sql
INSERT INTO TableName (ColumnName, TimestampColumn) VALUES ('Value', NOW());
```

Explanation of the Code:

- `INSERT INTO TableName (ColumnName, TimestampColumn) VALUES ('Value', NOW());`: In this code, we insert a new record into the "TableName" table. The "TimestampColumn" is populated with the current date and time provided by the NOW function. This records the timestamp of when the data was added.

Tips:

- The NOW function is particularly useful when you need to record the current timestamp in your database, especially for auditing purposes, tracking data modifications, or creating time-sensitive records.

- The actual datetime format and precision (including milliseconds) returned by NOW may vary depending on your database system. Be sure to understand how your database handles timestamp values.

- Be mindful of time zones when working with NOW. The returned timestamp may be in the time zone configured for your database.

- If you want to display the current timestamp in a specific format, you may need to use date formatting functions in conjunction with NOW, depending on your database system.

2.14 TIMESTAMPDIFF

Description:

The TIMESTAMPDIFF function in SQL is used to calculate the difference between two datetime or timestamp values and express it in a specified time unit (e.g., seconds, minutes, hours, days). It is commonly used for tasks that involve measuring the duration between two timestamps.

Syntax:

The syntax for the TIMESTAMPDIFF function is as follows:

```sql
TIMESTAMPDIFF(unit, datetime1, datetime2)
```

- `unit`: The time unit in which you want to express the difference (e.g., SECOND, MINUTE, HOUR, DAY, MONTH, YEAR).

- `datetime1`: The first datetime or timestamp value.

- `datetime2`: The second datetime or timestamp value.

Examples:

1. Calculate the Difference in Days:

To calculate the difference in days between two timestamps, you can use the TIMESTAMPDIFF function. For instance, to find the number of days between '2023-10-01' and '2023-10-15':

```sql
SELECT TIMESTAMPDIFF(DAY, '2023-10-01', '2023-10-15') AS DaysDifference;
```

```
```

Result: This query will return '14' as the difference in days between the two timestamps.

Explanation of the Code:

- `SELECT TIMESTAMPDIFF(DAY, '2023-10-01', '2023-10-15') AS DaysDifference`: This code calculates the difference in days between the two provided dates and stores it in the 'DaysDifference' column.

Tips:

- The TIMESTAMPDIFF function is versatile and can be used to measure the difference in various time units such as seconds, minutes, hours, days, months, and years.

- Ensure that the data type of the columns you are using with TIMESTAMPDIFF is datetime or timestamp types, as it expects valid datetime or timestamp values as input.

- Be mindful of the order of datetime values when using TIMESTAMPDIFF. The function calculates the difference as `datetime2 - datetime1`, so consider the order when measuring durations.

- Keep in mind that the result of TIMESTAMPDIFF will be an integer, representing the difference in the specified time unit. Adjust your queries accordingly to use the result as needed.

2.15 TIMESTAMPADD

Description:

The TIMESTAMPADD function in SQL is used to add a specified amount of time to a datetime or timestamp value. It is commonly used for tasks that involve adjusting timestamps, calculating future or past dates, and performing date arithmetic.

Syntax:

The syntax for the TIMESTAMPADD function is as follows:

```sql
TIMESTAMPADD(unit, quantity, datetime)
```

- `unit`: The time unit in which you want to add time (e.g., SECOND, MINUTE, HOUR, DAY, MONTH, YEAR).

- `quantity`: The amount of time to add, specified as an integer.

- `datetime`: The datetime or timestamp value to which you want to add time.

Examples:

1. Add 3 Months to a Date:

To add 3 months to a given date, you can use the TIMESTAMPADD function. For instance, to add 3 months to '2023-10-01':

```sql
SELECT TIMESTAMPADD(MONTH, 3, '2023-10-01') AS NewDate;
```

Result: This query will return '2024-01-01' as the result of adding 3 months to '2023-10-01'.

Explanation of the Code:

- `SELECT TIMESTAMPADD(MONTH, 3, '2023-10-01') AS NewDate`: This code adds 3 months to the provided date and stores the result in the 'NewDate' column.

Tips:

- The TIMESTAMPADD function is versatile and can be used to add time in various time units, including seconds, minutes, hours, days, months, and years.

- Ensure that the data type of the column you are using with TIMESTAMPADD is a datetime or timestamp type, as it expects valid datetime or timestamp values as input.

- Be cautious when adding time, as it may lead to invalid dates if not handled properly. For example, adding a large number of months could result in a date that does not exist (e.g., February 30th).

- Be aware of the order of the arguments in TIMESTAMPADD, as the function adds time to the provided datetime value.

- Consider using TIMESTAMPADD for tasks like calculating future or past dates, date-based projections, or adjusting timestamps for reporting and analysis.

2.16 DATE_FORMAT

Description:

The DATE_FORMAT function in SQL is used to format a date or datetime value into a specific string format. It allows you to convert a date or datetime value into a human-readable string with a customized format. DATE_FORMAT is commonly used for tasks that require displaying dates in a particular style for reporting or presentation.

Syntax:

The syntax for the DATE_FORMAT function is as follows:

```sql
DATE_FORMAT(date, format)
```

- `date`: The date or datetime value that you want to format.

- `format`: A format string specifying how you want the date to be displayed.

Examples:

1. Format a Date as "YYYY-MM-DD":

To format a date as "YYYY-MM-DD," you can use the DATE_FORMAT function. For instance, to format '2023-10-15' in this style:

```sql
SELECT DATE_FORMAT('2023-10-15', '%Y-%m-%d') AS FormattedDate;
```

Result: This query will return '2023-10-15' as the formatted date.

Explanation of the Code:

- `SELECT DATE_FORMAT('2023-10-15', '%Y-%m-%d') AS FormattedDate`: This code formats the provided date according to the specified format and stores the result in the 'FormattedDate' column.

Tips:

- The DATE_FORMAT function provides flexibility in customizing the date format using format codes. Common format codes include '%Y' for year, '%m' for month, '%d' for day, '%H' for hour, '%i' for minute, '%s' for second, etc. Refer to your database system's documentation for a full list of format codes.

- Be mindful of the order and case sensitivity of format codes. For example, '%Y' represents a four-digit year, while '%y' represents a two-digit year.

- Use DATE_FORMAT when you need to display dates in a specific format for reporting or user interfaces. It's a powerful tool for making dates more user-friendly.

- Take into account the locale and time zone settings of your database system, as they can affect the formatting of dates.

- Ensure that the 'date' input is a valid date or datetime value; otherwise, DATE_FORMAT may not produce the expected results.

2.17 STR_TO_DATE

Description:

The STR_TO_DATE function in SQL is used to convert a string representing a date or datetime into a valid date or datetime value. It is the opposite of the DATE_FORMAT function. STR_TO_DATE is commonly used when you have date information stored as strings and need to convert them into a date format for further manipulation or storage.

Syntax:

The syntax for the STR_TO_DATE function is as follows:

```sql
STR_TO_DATE(string, format)
```

- `string`: The string representing the date or datetime that you want to convert.

- `format`: A format string specifying how the date is represented in the input string.

Examples:

1. Convert a String to a Date:

To convert a string '2023-10-15' to a date, you can use the STR_TO_DATE function. For instance:

```sql
SELECT STR_TO_DATE('2023-10-15', '%Y-%m-%d') AS ConvertedDate;
```

Result: This query will return '2023-10-15' as the converted date.

Explanation of the Code:

- `SELECT STR_TO_DATE('2023-10-15', '%Y-%m-%d') AS ConvertedDate`: This code converts the provided string into a date according to the specified format and stores the result in the 'ConvertedDate' column.

Tips:

- The STR_TO_DATE function provides flexibility in specifying how the date is represented in the input string using format codes. Common format codes include '%Y' for year, '%m' for month, '%d' for day, '%H' for hour, '%i' for minute, '%s' for second, etc. Refer to your database system's documentation for a full list of format codes.

- Ensure that the format string used in STR_TO_DATE matches the format of the input string, or the conversion may not work as expected.

- Be cautious about the order and case sensitivity of format codes. For example, '%Y' represents a four-digit year, while '%y' represents a two-digit year.

- Use STR_TO_DATE when you have date information stored as strings and need to convert them into a date format for further processing or storage.

- Be aware of any potential data inconsistencies in the input strings, such as variations in date representation or invalid dates. Consider data validation and cleansing as needed.

2.18 CURDATE

Description:

The CURDATE function in SQL is used to retrieve the current date from the database system. It returns the current date as a date value. CURDATE is commonly used for tasks that require capturing the current date for various purposes, such as recording when data was added or performing date-based operations.

Syntax:

The syntax for the CURDATE function is simple. You call it as follows:

```sql
CURDATE()
```

Examples:

1. Retrieve the Current Date:

To retrieve the current date, you can use the CURDATE function. For instance, to capture the current date when a record is added to a table:

```sql
INSERT INTO TableName (ColumnName, DateColumn) VALUES ('Value', CURDATE());
```

Explanation of the Code:

- `INSERT INTO TableName (ColumnName, DateColumn) VALUES ('Value', CURDATE());`: In this code, we insert a new record into the "TableName" table. The "DateColumn" is populated with the current date provided by the CURDATE function, recording the date when the data was added.

Tips:

- The CURDATE function is particularly useful when you need to record the current date in your database, especially for auditing purposes, tracking data additions, or creating time-sensitive records.

- Ensure that the data type of the column you are using with CURDATE is a date type, as it expects a valid date as output.

- Be aware of the date format used by your database system, as it can affect the interpretation of the current date provided by CURDATE.

- CURDATE provides the current date without the time component. If you need both the date and time, you can use the NOW function or other datetime functions.

- Use CURDATE when you only need the current date without the time information.

2.19 CURTIME

Description:

The CURTIME function in SQL is used to retrieve the current time from the database system. It returns the current time as a time value. CURTIME is commonly used for tasks that require capturing the current time for various purposes, such as recording when data was added or performing time-based operations.

Syntax:

The syntax for the CURTIME function is straightforward. You call it as follows:

```sql
CURTIME()
```

Examples:

1. Retrieve the Current Time:

To retrieve the current time, you can use the CURTIME function. For instance, to capture the current time when a record is added to a table:

```sql
INSERT INTO TableName (ColumnName, TimeColumn) VALUES ('Value', CURTIME());
```

Explanation of the Code:

- `INSERT INTO TableName (ColumnName, TimeColumn) VALUES ('Value', CURTIME());`: In this code, we insert a new record into the "TableName" table. The "TimeColumn" is populated with the current time provided by the CURTIME function, recording the time when the data was added.

Tips:

- The CURTIME function is particularly useful when you need to record the current time in your database, especially for auditing purposes, tracking data additions, or creating time-sensitive records.

- Ensure that the data type of the column you are using with CURTIME is a time type, as it expects a valid time as output.

- Be aware of the time format used by your database system, as it can affect the interpretation of the current time provided by CURTIME.

- CURTIME provides the current time without the date component. If you need both the date and time, you can use the NOW function or other datetime functions.

- Use CURTIME when you only need the current time without the date information.

2.20 EXTRACT

Description:

The EXTRACT function in SQL is used to extract a specific component, such as year, month, day, or time, from a date or timestamp value. It allows you to break down a date or timestamp into its individual parts, making it useful for date-based analysis and reporting.

Syntax:

The syntax for the EXTRACT function is as follows:

```sql
EXTRACT(unit FROM datetime)
```

- `unit`: The specific component you want to extract, such as YEAR, MONTH, DAY, HOUR, etc.

- `datetime`: The date or timestamp value from which you want to extract the component.

Examples:

1. Extract the Year from a Date:

To extract the year from a date, you can use the EXTRACT function. For instance, to extract the year from '2023-10-15':

```sql
SELECT EXTRACT(YEAR FROM '2023-10-15') AS ExtractedYear;
```

Result: This query will return '2023' as the extracted year.

Explanation of the Code:

- `SELECT EXTRACT(YEAR FROM '2023-10-15') AS ExtractedYear`: This code extracts the year component from the provided date and stores the result in the 'ExtractedYear' column.

Tips:

- The EXTRACT function is flexible and allows you to extract various components, including years, months, days, hours, minutes, and more. The choice of 'unit' determines what component you want to extract.

- Be aware that the 'unit' argument in EXTRACT is case-insensitive in most database systems. For example, 'YEAR' and 'year' are both valid.

- When using EXTRACT, make sure that the 'datetime' input is a valid date or timestamp value, as it expects such inputs.

- EXTRACT is particularly useful when you need to perform date-based analysis, group data by date components, or calculate time-related metrics.

- Check your database system's documentation for a full list of supported 'unit' values and the format of the extracted components.

III.
Conditional functions and Operators

3.1 CASE

Description:

The CASE function in SQL is used for conditional logic, allowing you to perform different actions based on specific conditions. It is similar to the "if-then-else" logic in programming languages. You can use CASE to evaluate conditions and return different values or perform different actions based on the result of the evaluation.

Syntax:

The syntax for the CASE function can take two forms: the simple CASE and the searched CASE.

1. Simple CASE:

```sql
CASE expression

    WHEN value1 THEN result1

    WHEN value2 THEN result2

    ...

    ELSE default_result

END
```

```

**2. Searched CASE:**

```sql
CASE
    WHEN condition1 THEN result1
    WHEN condition2 THEN result2
    ...
    ELSE default_result
END
```

- `expression`: The value or expression that is evaluated in a simple CASE.
- `value1`, `value2`, etc.: The values to compare with the `expression` in a simple CASE.
- `condition1`, `condition2`, etc.: The conditions to evaluate in a searched CASE.
- `result1`, `result2`, etc.: The results to return when the condition is true.
- `default_result`: The result to return if no conditions are met.

Examples:

1. Simple CASE:

To categorize employees based on their salary ranges, you can use a simple CASE. For instance:

```sql
```
```

```sql
SELECT
    EmployeeName,
    CASE
        WHEN Salary < 30000 THEN 'Low'
        WHEN Salary < 60000 THEN 'Medium'
        ELSE 'High'
    END AS SalaryCategory
FROM Employees;
```

Result: This query will categorize employees into 'Low,' 'Medium,' or 'High' based on their salaries.

Explanation of the Code:

- The CASE expression evaluates the employee's salary.

- Depending on the salary range, it returns a corresponding category, and the result is stored in the 'SalaryCategory' column.

Tips:

- CASE is a powerful tool for creating conditional expressions within SQL queries.

- You can use both simple and searched CASE statements based on your specific needs.

- Always include an `ELSE` clause in your CASE statement to handle conditions that do not match any of the specified cases.

- You can nest CASE statements within other CASE statements for more complex logic.

- Be mindful of the order of evaluation; CASE stops when it finds the first true condition in order, so put the most specific conditions first.

- CASE is commonly used in SELECT, WHERE, and ORDER BY clauses, but it can be used in other parts of SQL statements as well.

3.2 IF

Description:

In SQL, the IF function is typically not a built-in function. Instead, it is often implemented using various conditional constructs provided by different database management systems (DBMS) such as MySQL, SQL Server, or PostgreSQL. The purpose of the IF function is to provide conditional logic, similar to the CASE function. It allows you to perform different actions based on specific conditions.

Syntax (MySQL):

The syntax for the IF function in MySQL is as follows:

```sql
IF(condition, value_if_true, value_if_false)
```

- `condition`: The condition to evaluate. If this condition is true, the function returns `value_if_true`; otherwise, it returns `value_if_false`.

- `value_if_true`: The value or expression to return if the condition is true.

- `value_if_false`: The value or expression to return if the condition is false.

Example (MySQL):

To categorize employees based on their salary ranges using MySQL's IF function:

```sql
SELECT
  EmployeeName,
```

IF(Salary < 30000, 'Low', IF(Salary < 60000, 'Medium', 'High')) AS SalaryCategory

FROM Employees;

```

**Explanation of the Code:**

- The IF function evaluates the condition `Salary < 30000`. If true, it returns 'Low.' If false, it evaluates the next condition, and so on.

- This nested IF function categorizes employees into 'Low,' 'Medium,' or 'High' based on their salaries.


**Tips:**

- The availability and syntax of the IF function may vary depending on the DBMS you are using. For example, in SQL Server, you can use the IIF function with a similar purpose.

- When using the IF function, consider nesting IF statements for more complex conditional logic.

- Ensure that you handle all possible conditions, including the `ELSE` condition, to avoid unexpected results.

- Pay attention to the data types of the values returned by the IF function, as they should be compatible.

- SQL's CASE function is a more commonly used construct for performing conditional operations, and it is more portable across different database systems. Use the CASE function when possible.
```

3.3 COALESCE

Description:

The COALESCE function in SQL is used to return the first non-null expression from a list of expressions. It is often used to handle situations where you have multiple values and want to retrieve the first non-null value. COALESCE is particularly useful in scenarios where you need to provide a default value when there are null values in the data.

Syntax:

The syntax for the COALESCE function is as follows:

```sql
COALESCE(expr1, expr2, expr3, ...)
```

- `expr1`, `expr2`, `expr3`, etc.: A list of expressions to evaluate. The function returns the first non-null expression from this list.

Example:

To retrieve a person's preferred name, using COALESCE to handle null values:

```sql
SELECT
    FirstName,
    COALESCE(Nickname, MiddleName, FirstName) AS PreferredName
FROM People;
```

Explanation of the Code:

- In this query, we're trying to find a person's preferred name.

- We use COALESCE to check the Nickname, MiddleName, and FirstName in order. The first non-null name is returned as the PreferredName.

Tips:

- COALESCE is particularly useful when dealing with scenarios where you have multiple columns or expressions and want to retrieve the first non-null value.

- It is often used in SELECT statements to handle default values, but you can use it in other parts of SQL statements as well.

- The COALESCE function may not be available in all database systems, but similar functionality can often be achieved using other functions, such as ISNULL in SQL Server or IFNULL in MySQL.

- Be cautious with the order of expressions in COALESCE. The function returns the first non-null value it encounters, so place the most preferred option first in the list.

- COALESCE is helpful for making SQL queries more robust by ensuring that you always have a valid value, even when some data is missing or null.

3.4 NULLIF

Description:

The NULLIF function in SQL is used to compare two expressions and return null if they are equal, or return the first expression if they are not equal. It is particularly useful when you want to handle cases where two expressions might be equal, and you want to replace such cases with null.

Syntax:

The syntax for the NULLIF function is as follows:

```sql
NULLIF(expression1, expression2)
```

- `expression1`: The first expression to compare.

- `expression2`: The second expression to compare.

Example:

To return null when the quantity is zero using the NULLIF function:

```sql
SELECT ProductName, NULLIF(Quantity, 0) AS AvailableQuantity
FROM Products;
```

Explanation of the Code:

- In this query, we want to show the available quantity for each product.

- We use the NULLIF function to compare the Quantity with zero. If the Quantity is zero, it returns null, indicating that the product is not available. If the Quantity is not zero, it returns the actual Quantity.

Tips:

- NULLIF is handy when you want to replace a specific value with null in your query results.

- It's often used in SELECT statements but can also be used in other parts of SQL statements.

- Be careful with data types when using NULLIF; the two expressions being compared should have compatible data types.

- NULLIF can make your query results more informative and user-friendly by handling cases where certain values should be treated as null.

- Use NULLIF when you need to replace specific values with null, and use COALESCE when you want to find the first non-null value from a list of expressions.

3.5 IS NULL

Description:

The IS NULL operator in SQL is used to check if a column or an expression contains a NULL value. It returns true if the value is NULL and false if it's not. It's a simple and essential tool for handling and querying databases where NULL values can be present.

Syntax:

The syntax for the IS NULL operator is as follows:

```sql
column_name IS NULL
```

- `column_name`: The name of the column or the expression you want to check for NULL.

Example:

To find all employees with missing email addresses using the IS NULL operator:

```sql
SELECT EmployeeName
FROM Employees
WHERE EmailAddress IS NULL;
```

Explanation of the Code:

- In this query, we want to find all employees who don't have an email address.

- The `WHERE` clause uses the IS NULL operator to filter rows where the EmailAddress column is NULL.

Tips:

- The IS NULL operator is a simple yet crucial tool for working with NULL values in SQL databases.

- It's commonly used in `SELECT`, `WHERE`, and `JOIN` statements to filter or identify rows with missing or NULL data.

- Be cautious when using IS NULL. Remember that it only checks for NULL values and not for other types of missing data, such as empty strings or default values.

- If you want to check for non-NULL values, you can use the IS NOT NULL operator.

- When querying databases, consider the presence of NULL values and how to handle them in your results, whether by using IS NULL or by providing default values.

3.6 IS NOT NULL

Description:

The IS NOT NULL operator in SQL is used to check if a column or an expression does not contain a NULL value. It returns true if the value is not NULL and false if it is. This operator is useful when you want to filter rows that have non-NULL values in a specific column or expression.

Syntax:

The syntax for the IS NOT NULL operator is as follows:

```sql
column_name IS NOT NULL
```

- `column_name`: The name of the column or the expression you want to check for non-NULL values.

Example:

To find all employees with valid email addresses (i.e., not NULL) using the IS NOT NULL operator:

```sql
SELECT EmployeeName
FROM Employees
WHERE EmailAddress IS NOT NULL;
```

Explanation of the Code:

- In this query, we want to find all employees who have a valid (non-NULL) email address.

- The `WHERE` clause uses the IS NOT NULL operator to filter rows where the EmailAddress column is not NULL.

Tips:

- The IS NOT NULL operator is a fundamental tool for identifying and filtering rows with non-NULL values in SQL databases.

- It's commonly used in `SELECT`, `WHERE`, and `JOIN` statements to work with non-NULL data.

- Be mindful of the data quality in your database and how NULL values are handled. IS NOT NULL is particularly useful when you want to ensure that you're working with complete and valid data.

- Remember that IS NOT NULL only checks for non-NULL values. It does not guarantee the data's accuracy or validity. Always consider your data quality and data validation practices.

- When querying databases, take into account how to handle both NULL and non-NULL values, depending on your specific needs and business rules.

3.7 BETWEEN

Description:

The BETWEEN operator in SQL is used to filter rows based on a specified range of values. It checks if a value falls within a specified range, inclusive of the endpoints. The BETWEEN operator is often used in conjunction with the `WHERE` clause to retrieve rows that meet certain criteria within a defined range.

Syntax:

The syntax for the BETWEEN operator is as follows:

```sql
value BETWEEN low_value AND high_value
```

- `value`: The value you want to compare.

- `low_value`: The lower endpoint of the range.

- `high_value`: The upper endpoint of the range.

Example:

To find all products with a price between $10 and $50 using the BETWEEN operator:

```sql
SELECT ProductName, Price
FROM Products
WHERE Price BETWEEN 10 AND 50;
```

Explanation of the Code:

- In this query, we want to retrieve products that fall within the price range of $10 to $50.

- The `WHERE` clause uses the BETWEEN operator to filter rows where the Price column is between 10 and 50, inclusive.

Tips:

- The BETWEEN operator simplifies range-based filtering in SQL, making it easier to work with continuous data ranges like dates, numbers, or prices.

- When using BETWEEN, be mindful of the endpoints. It is inclusive, so it will include rows with values equal to `low_value` and `high_value`.

- Be aware of the data types when using BETWEEN. Ensure that the data types of `value`, `low_value`, and `high_value` are compatible and represent the same type of data (e.g., numbers, dates, or strings).

- You can use the `NOT BETWEEN` operator to find rows that fall outside the specified range.

- When working with date ranges, consider that the time component may also be included in the comparison if it is part of the date values.

- The BETWEEN operator is a powerful tool for creating more precise and focused queries in SQL.

3.8 IN

Description:

The IN operator in SQL is used to filter rows based on a set of specified values. It checks if a value matches any value in a given list of values. The IN operator is commonly used in conjunction with the `WHERE` clause to filter rows that have values within a specific set.

Syntax:

The syntax for the IN operator is as follows:

```sql
value IN (value1, value2, value3, ...)
```

- `value`: The value you want to compare.

- `value1, value2, value3, ...`: A list of values to compare against.

Example:

To find all products with a certain category using the IN operator:

```sql
SELECT ProductName, Category
FROM Products
WHERE Category IN ('Electronics', 'Clothing', 'Books');
```

Explanation of the Code:

- In this query, we want to retrieve products that belong to specific categories.

- The `WHERE` clause uses the IN operator to filter rows where the Category matches any of the specified values ('Electronics', 'Clothing', 'Books').

Tips:

- The IN operator simplifies filtering for multiple values and is especially useful when you want to match against a predefined list or set.

- When using IN, the list of values should be enclosed in parentheses, and individual values should be separated by commas.

- Be cautious about the data types of the values being compared. The data type of the `value` should be compatible with the data types in the list.

- You can also use NOT IN to find rows that do not match any of the specified values.

- The IN operator is a versatile tool for filtering data based on predefined sets or lists. It's commonly used in scenarios where you want to retrieve data that falls into specific categories, types, or groups.

- When using the IN operator with a large list of values, it's essential to optimize your query for performance to ensure it runs efficiently.

3.9 LIKE

Description:

The LIKE operator in SQL is used to search for a specified pattern within a text column. It allows you to perform pattern matching, where you can use wildcards to represent one or more characters. This is particularly useful for finding data that partially matches a search string or pattern.

Syntax:

The syntax for the LIKE operator is as follows:

```sql
column_name LIKE pattern
```

- `column_name`: The name of the column where you want to search for a pattern.

- `pattern`: The pattern you want to search for, which can include wildcards.

Wildcards in the pattern:

- `%`: Represents zero, one, or multiple characters.

- `_`: Represents a single character.

Example:

To find all customers with names starting with "J" using the LIKE operator:

```sql
SELECT CustomerName
```

FROM Customers

WHERE CustomerName LIKE 'J%';

```

**Explanation of the Code:**

- In this query, we want to find customers whose names start with the letter "J."

- The `WHERE` clause uses the LIKE operator with the pattern 'J%' to match names that begin with "J."

**Tips:**

- The LIKE operator is a powerful tool for searching and filtering text data.

- The % wildcard is often used at the end of a pattern to match all text following a specific character or sequence.

- The _ wildcard is used to match a single character at a specific position within the pattern.

- You can use multiple wildcards in a pattern to create more complex searches.

- Be mindful of case sensitivity when using LIKE. Some database systems are case-sensitive, so 'A' and 'a' might not match.

- LIKE can be used with not only letters but also numbers, special characters, and symbols to search for specific patterns in text data.

- Avoid using LIKE with patterns that start with a wildcard (%) because it can lead to inefficient queries that scan the entire column.

- Use the "ESCAPE" clause to escape special characters when you want to search for them as literal characters.
```

3.10 NOT LIKE

Description:

The NOT LIKE operator in SQL is used to search for rows that do not match a specified pattern within a text column. It is the negation of the LIKE operator. NOT LIKE is commonly used to exclude rows that match a particular pattern from the result set.

Syntax:

The syntax for the NOT LIKE operator is as follows:

```sql
column_name NOT LIKE pattern
```

- `column_name`: The name of the column where you want to search for a pattern.

- `pattern`: The pattern you want to exclude from the result set.

Wildcards in the pattern:

- `%`: Represents zero, one, or multiple characters.

- `_`: Represents a single character.

Example:

To find all customers with names that do not start with "J" using the NOT LIKE operator:

```sql
SELECT CustomerName
```

```
FROM Customers
WHERE CustomerName NOT LIKE 'J%';
```

Explanation of the Code:

- In this query, we want to find customers whose names do not start with the letter "J."

- The `WHERE` clause uses the NOT LIKE operator with the pattern 'J%' to exclude names that begin with "J."

Tips:

- The NOT LIKE operator is particularly useful for excluding specific patterns from your query results.

- You can use it to filter out rows that match a particular pattern while retaining those that do not match.

- Be mindful of case sensitivity when using NOT LIKE. Some database systems are case-sensitive, so 'A' and 'a' might not match.

- Use appropriate wildcards, such as % and _, in the pattern to create more refined exclusions.

- Avoid using NOT LIKE with patterns that start with a wildcard (%) because it can lead to inefficient queries that scan the entire column.

- When using NOT LIKE, you are excluding rows that match the specified pattern, so you can get a result set with all other rows that do not match.

3.11 EXISTS

Description:

The EXISTS operator in SQL is used to check for the existence of rows in a subquery's result set. It returns TRUE if the subquery returns at least one row, and FALSE if the subquery returns no rows. EXISTS is often used in combination with the `SELECT` statement, primarily within the `WHERE` clause.

Syntax:

The syntax for the EXISTS operator is as follows:

```sql
EXISTS (subquery)
```

- `subquery`: A valid SQL query that returns a result set.

Example:

To find all orders placed by customers with outstanding balances using the EXISTS operator:

```sql
SELECT OrderID, CustomerID
FROM Orders
WHERE EXISTS (SELECT 1 FROM Customers WHERE Customers.CustomerID = Orders.CustomerID AND Customers.Balance > 1000);
```

Explanation of the Code:

- In this query, we want to retrieve orders placed by customers with outstanding balances (greater than 1000).

- The `WHERE` clause uses the EXISTS operator with a subquery that checks if there's at least one row in the Customers table that matches the condition (CustomerID = Orders.CustomerID and Balance > 1000).

Tips:

- The EXISTS operator is useful for performing correlated subqueries, where the subquery references columns from the outer query.

- It is more efficient than using COUNT(*) to check for the existence of rows in a subquery because EXISTS stops processing once it finds a matching row.

- Use EXISTS when you need to filter rows in the main query based on a condition in the subquery.

- Be cautious when using EXISTS in subqueries, as improper usage can lead to unexpected results. Ensure that your subquery is properly correlated with the main query.

- You can use NOT EXISTS to check for the non-existence of rows in a subquery.

- EXISTS is often used with table relationships and is valuable for filtering data based on related records' presence or absence.

3.12 NOT EXISTS

Description:

The NOT EXISTS operator in SQL is used to check for the non-existence of rows in a subquery's result set. It returns TRUE if the subquery returns no rows, and FALSE if the subquery returns at least one row. NOT EXISTS is often used in combination with the `SELECT` statement, primarily within the `WHERE` clause.

Syntax:

The syntax for the NOT EXISTS operator is as follows:

```sql
NOT EXISTS (subquery)
```

- `subquery`: A valid SQL query that returns a result set.

Example:

To find all customers who have not placed any orders using the NOT EXISTS operator:

```sql
SELECT CustomerName
FROM Customers
WHERE NOT EXISTS (SELECT 1 FROM Orders WHERE Orders.CustomerID = Customers.CustomerID);
```

Explanation of the Code:

- In this query, we want to retrieve customers who have not placed any orders.

- The `WHERE` clause uses the NOT EXISTS operator with a subquery that checks if there are no rows in the Orders table that match the condition (CustomerID = Customers.CustomerID).

Tips:

- The NOT EXISTS operator is useful for performing correlated subqueries, where the subquery references columns from the outer query.

- It is more efficient than using COUNT(*) to check for the non-existence of rows in a subquery because NOT EXISTS stops processing once it finds a matching row.

- Use NOT EXISTS when you need to filter rows in the main query based on the absence of a condition in the subquery.

- Be cautious when using NOT EXISTS in subqueries, as improper usage can lead to unexpected results. Ensure that your subquery is properly correlated with the main query.

- You can use EXISTS to check for the existence of rows in a subquery.

- NOT EXISTS is often used with table relationships and is valuable for filtering data based on the absence of related records.

3.13 ALL

Description:

The ALL operator in SQL is used to compare a value to all values returned by a subquery. It is often used in combination with comparison operators to determine if a value satisfies a condition for all rows in the subquery's result set.

Syntax:

The syntax for the ALL operator is as follows:

```sql
expression operator ALL (subquery)
```

- `expression`: The value you want to compare with all values from the subquery.

- `operator`: A comparison operator (e.g., =, <, >, <=, >=, <>) used to compare the expression with the values in the subquery.

- `subquery`: A valid SQL query that returns a result set of values to be compared.

Example:

To find employees whose salaries are greater than or equal to all salaries in the Sales department using the ALL operator:

```sql
SELECT EmployeeName
FROM Employees
WHERE Salary >= ALL (SELECT Salary FROM Employees WHERE Department = 'Sales');
```

Explanation of the Code:

- In this query, we want to retrieve employees whose salaries are greater than or equal to all salaries in the Sales department.

- The `WHERE` clause uses the ALL operator with a subquery that checks if the Salary of the employee is greater than or equal to all the salaries in the Sales department.

Tips:

- The ALL operator is often used with comparison operators to compare a single value to multiple values in a subquery.

- Be careful with the choice of the comparison operator. It determines how the expression is compared to the values in the subquery (e.g., greater than, less than, equal to, etc.).

- Ensure that the subquery returns a list of values that can be compared to the expression.

- You can also use the ANY operator to compare a value to at least one value in the subquery's result set.

- The subquery should return a single column with values that can be compared to the expression.

- Use the ALL operator when you need to check if a condition is true for all rows in the subquery's result set.

3.14 ANY / SOME

Description:

The ANY and SOME functions in SQL are used to compare a value to any or some values returned by a subquery. They are often used in combination with comparison operators to determine if a value satisfies a condition for at least one row in the subquery's result set.

Syntax:

The syntax for the ANY and SOME functions is as follows:

```sql
expression operator ANY (subquery)
```

- `expression`: The value you want to compare with some or any values from the subquery.

- `operator`: A comparison operator (e.g., =, <, >, <=, >=, <>) used to compare the expression with the values in the subquery.

- `subquery`: A valid SQL query that returns a result set of values to be compared.

Example:

To find employees whose salaries are greater than or equal to any salary in the Sales department using the ANY or SOME operator:

```sql
SELECT EmployeeName
FROM Employees
WHERE Salary >= ANY (SELECT Salary FROM Employees WHERE Department = 'Sales');
```

Explanation of the Code:

- In this query, we want to retrieve employees whose salaries are greater than or equal to at least one salary in the Sales department.

- The `WHERE` clause uses the ANY or SOME operator with a subquery that checks if the Salary of the employee is greater than or equal to at least one salary in the Sales department.

Tips:

- The ANY and SOME operators are often used with comparison operators to compare a single value to multiple values in a subquery.

- Be careful with the choice of the comparison operator. It determines how the expression is compared to the values in the subquery (e.g., greater than, less than, equal to, etc.).

- Ensure that the subquery returns a list of values that can be compared to the expression.

- You can use either ANY or SOME; they are equivalent in functionality.

- The subquery should return a single column with values that can be compared to the expression.

- Use ANY or SOME when you need to check if a condition is true for at least one row in the subquery's result set.

3.15 AND

Description:

The AND operator in SQL is a logical operator that combines two or more Boolean conditions. It returns true only if all the conditions specified are true. It is often used in the WHERE clause to filter rows that meet multiple criteria.

Syntax:

The syntax for the AND operator is as follows:

```sql
condition1 AND condition2
```

- `condition1` and `condition2`: Boolean expressions or conditions that you want to combine. They can be column comparisons, logical expressions, or any conditions that evaluate to true or false.

Example:

Suppose you have a table named "Students" with columns "Age" and "Grade." You want to retrieve students who are both older than 18 years and have a grade higher than or equal to 80:

```sql
SELECT * FROM Students
WHERE Age > 18 AND Grade >= 80;
```

Explanation of the Code:

- In this query, the WHERE clause uses the AND operator to combine two conditions: Age > 18 and Grade >= 80.

- The query will retrieve students who meet both conditions simultaneously.

Tips:

- Use the AND operator to filter rows based on multiple conditions that all need to be true.

- You can combine more than two conditions using multiple AND operators (e.g., condition1 AND condition2 AND condition3).

- Be careful with parentheses when combining multiple logical operators, especially when using both AND and OR together, to ensure the desired logic is achieved.

- The AND operator follows the short-circuit evaluation, meaning if the first condition is false, the second condition will not be evaluated. This can be useful for performance optimization in some cases.

- Consider using parentheses to explicitly define the order of evaluation if your query involves a mix of AND and OR operators to avoid confusion and ensure the desired logic.

3.16 OR

Description:

The OR operator in SQL is a logical operator that combines two or more Boolean conditions. It returns true if at least one of the conditions specified is true. It is often used in the WHERE clause to filter rows that meet any of multiple criteria.

Syntax:

The syntax for the OR operator is as follows:

```sql
condition1 OR condition2
```

- `condition1` and `condition2`: Boolean expressions or conditions that you want to combine. They can be column comparisons, logical expressions, or any conditions that evaluate to true or false.

Example:

Suppose you have a table named "Products" with columns "Category" and "Price." You want to retrieve products that belong to the "Electronics" category or have a price lower than $200:

```sql
SELECT * FROM Products
WHERE Category = 'Electronics' OR Price < 200;
```

Explanation of the Code:

- In this query, the WHERE clause uses the OR operator to combine two conditions: Category = 'Electronics' and Price < 200.

- The query will retrieve products that meet either of the conditions.

Tips:

- Use the OR operator to filter rows based on multiple conditions where at least one condition needs to be true.

- You can combine more than two conditions using multiple OR operators (e.g., condition1 OR condition2 OR condition3).

- Be careful with parentheses when combining multiple logical operators, especially when using both AND and OR together, to ensure the desired logic is achieved.

- The OR operator follows the short-circuit evaluation, meaning if the first condition is true, the second condition will not be evaluated. This can be useful for performance optimization in some cases.

- Consider using parentheses to explicitly define the order of evaluation if your query involves a mix of AND and OR operators to avoid confusion and ensure the desired logic.

3.17 NOT

Description:

The NOT operator in SQL is a logical operator used to reverse the truth value of a Boolean expression. It is typically used to negate a condition, making a true condition false and vice versa. NOT is often used in combination with other logical operators (e.g., NOT AND, NOT OR) to create complex conditions.

Syntax:

The syntax for the NOT operator is as follows:

```sql
NOT condition
```

- `condition`: A Boolean expression or condition that you want to negate. It can be a column comparison, logical expression, or any condition that evaluates to true or false.

Example:

Suppose you have a table named "Customers" with a column "IsPremium" indicating whether a customer has a premium account (1 for premium, 0 for non-premium). You want to retrieve all non-premium customers:

```sql
SELECT * FROM Customers
WHERE NOT IsPremium = 1;
```

Explanation of the Code:

- In this query, the WHERE clause uses the NOT operator to negate the condition IsPremium = 1.

- The query will retrieve all customers who are not premium.

Tips:

- Use the NOT operator to reverse the truth value of a condition. It turns true into false and false into true.

- NOT can be combined with other logical operators to create complex conditions. For example, NOT AND, NOT OR, etc.

- Parentheses can be used to control the order of evaluation when combining NOT with other operators, especially in complex conditions.

- Be cautious when using NOT in conjunction with NULL values. NOT NULL is not the same as FALSE; it's treated as an unknown value, so the result may not always be as expected.

IV.
Encryption, Hashing and Operations functions

4.1 ENCRYPT

Description:

The ENCRYPT function in SQL is used to encrypt data, typically sensitive information like passwords or personal information, to protect it from unauthorized access. It takes a plaintext value and a key as input and returns the encrypted result. Encryption ensures data confidentiality and security.

Syntax:

The syntax for the ENCRYPT function can vary depending on the SQL database system being used. Different database systems may have different encryption algorithms and key management. Here's a generic representation:

```sql
ENCRYPT(plaintext, key)
```

- `plaintext`: The data you want to encrypt.

- `key`: The encryption key used to perform the encryption.

Example:

Suppose you want to encrypt a password before storing it in a database using a hypothetical ENCRYPT function. Here's how it might be used:

```sql
-- Assuming ENCRYPT('myPassword', 'encryptionKey') encrypts 'myPassword' with the key 'encryptionKey'

INSERT INTO Users (Username, Password)

VALUES ('john_doe', ENCRYPT('myPassword', 'encryptionKey'));
```

Explanation of the Code:

- In this example, the ENCRYPT function is used to encrypt the password 'myPassword' using the encryption key 'encryptionKey'.

- The encrypted result is then inserted into a Users table, associating it with the username 'john_doe.'

Tips:

- Always use strong encryption algorithms and ensure that encryption keys are securely managed.

- Be cautious with storing encryption keys; they should be stored separately from the encrypted data to enhance security.

- Consider using built-in encryption functions or libraries provided by your database system for better security and compatibility.

- Ensure that the encrypted data can be properly decrypted when needed, using the same key and algorithm used for encryption.

- It's important to follow best practices for data security, especially when dealing with sensitive information.

4.2 DECRYPT

Description:

The DECRYPT function in SQL is used to decrypt data that has been previously encrypted. It takes an encrypted value and the decryption key as input and returns the original plaintext data. Decryption is performed to recover sensitive information or other data that was encrypted for security purposes.

Syntax:

The syntax for the DECRYPT function can vary depending on the SQL database system being used. Different database systems may have different decryption algorithms and key management. Here's a generic representation:

```sql
DECRYPT(encrypted_data, decryption_key)
```

- `encrypted_data`: The data that you want to decrypt.

- `decryption_key`: The key used to perform the decryption.

Example:

Suppose you have previously encrypted a password using the hypothetical ENCRYPT function, and you want to retrieve the original plaintext password:

```sql
```

-- Assuming DECRYPT(encryptedPassword, 'encryptionKey') decrypts 'encryptedPassword' with the key 'encryptionKey'

SELECT DECRYPT(Password, 'encryptionKey') AS DecryptedPassword

FROM Users

WHERE Username = 'john_doe';

```

**Explanation of the Code:**

- In this example, the DECRYPT function is used to decrypt the 'Password' stored in the 'Users' table for the user 'john_doe.'

- The decryption key 'encryptionKey' is used to retrieve the original plaintext password.

- The result is returned as 'DecryptedPassword.'

**Tips:**

- Always use the correct decryption key that was used during encryption.

- Ensure that the decryption key is kept secure and separate from the encrypted data.

- Verify the compatibility of encryption and decryption algorithms to ensure successful data recovery.

- Be careful when handling sensitive data and use encryption and decryption in accordance with data security best practices.

- Follow recommended guidelines for data protection and compliance with data privacy regulations.
```

4.3 HASHBYTES

Description:

The HASHBYTES function in SQL is used to generate a fixed-size binary hash value based on the input string. It is commonly used for hashing sensitive information such as passwords and verifying data integrity. The most commonly supported hashing algorithms are MD2, MD4, MD5, SHA, and others, depending on the database system.

Syntax:

The syntax for the HASHBYTES function can vary depending on the SQL database system being used. Different systems support different hashing algorithms. Here's a generic representation:

```sql
HASHBYTES('algorithm', input_string)
```

- `'algorithm'`: Specifies the hashing algorithm to use (e.g., 'MD5', 'SHA1', etc.).

- `input_string`: The string you want to hash.

Example:

Suppose you want to hash a user's password using the MD5 algorithm:

```sql
-- Assuming MD5 is a supported hashing algorithm
```

```
SELECT HASHBYTES('MD5', 'user_password') AS HashedPassword;
```

Explanation of the Code:

- In this example, the HASHBYTES function is used to hash the string 'user_password' using the MD5 hashing algorithm.

- The result is returned as 'HashedPassword.'

Tips:

- Choose a secure and cryptographically strong hashing algorithm based on your security requirements.

- Ensure that the input data is salted (if necessary) before hashing to protect against rainbow table attacks.

- Store the hash value securely, and never store plain text passwords or sensitive data.

- When verifying data integrity, compare the stored hash value with the newly generated hash value to detect any changes.

- Be aware that different SQL database systems may support different hashing algorithms, so check your system's documentation for available options.

4.4 ENCRYPTBYPASSPHRASE

Description:

The ENCRYPTBYPASSPHRASE function in SQL is used for data encryption with a passphrase. It encrypts sensitive data using a passphrase as the key, making it a useful tool for protecting confidential information. It's often used in scenarios where data security is a priority.

Syntax:

The syntax for the ENCRYPTBYPASSPHRASE function typically includes two parameters:

```sql
ENCRYPTBYPASSPHRASE('passphrase', input_string)
```

- `'passphrase'`: A passphrase or password that serves as the encryption key.
- `input_string`: The string or data you want to encrypt.

Example:

Suppose you want to encrypt a social security number (SSN) using a passphrase:

```sql
DECLARE @Passphrase NVARCHAR(50) = 'MySecretPassphrase';
DECLARE @SSN NVARCHAR(11) = '123-45-6789';
```

```
-- Encrypt SSN

SELECT ENCRYPTBYPASSPHRASE(@Passphrase, @SSN) AS EncryptedSSN;

```

Explanation of the Code:

- In this example, a passphrase 'MySecretPassphrase' is defined and stored in the variable `@Passphrase`.

- The SSN '123-45-6789' is stored in the variable `@SSN`.

- The ENCRYPTBYPASSPHRASE function is used to encrypt the SSN using the provided passphrase.

- The result is returned as 'EncryptedSSN'.

Tips:

- Choose a strong passphrase or password to ensure the security of the encryption.

- Protect and manage the passphrase carefully, as it is the key to decrypt the data.

- Ensure that the encryption algorithm and key management practices align with your organization's security policies and compliance requirements.

- When decrypting data, use the DECRYPTBYPASSPHRASE function with the same passphrase to retrieve the original data.

- Be aware of performance considerations when encrypting large amounts of data, as encryption and decryption can be resource-intensive operations.

4.5 DECRYPTBYPASSPHRASE

Description:

The DECRYPTBYPASSPHRASE function in SQL is used to decrypt data that has been encrypted using the ENCRYPTBYPASSPHRASE function. It requires the same passphrase used for encryption to decrypt the data. DECRYPTBYPASSPHRASE is often used for retrieving encrypted data in its original form.

Syntax:

The syntax for the DECRYPTBYPASSPHRASE function typically includes two parameters:

```sql
DECRYPTBYPASSPHRASE('passphrase', encrypted_string)
```

- `'passphrase'`: The same passphrase or password used for encryption.
- `encrypted_string`: The encrypted data that you want to decrypt.

Example:

Suppose you want to decrypt an SSN that was previously encrypted with a passphrase:

```sql
DECLARE @Passphrase NVARCHAR(50) = 'MySecretPassphrase';

DECLARE @EncryptedSSN VARBINARY(MAX) =
0x0100000078030000002F19C5AA5FD4F08F3A6C1A4E71D15899A3C9B899EA573A3;
```

-- Decrypt SSN

SELECT CAST(DECRYPTBYPASSPHRASE(@Passphrase, @EncryptedSSN) AS
NVARCHAR(11)) AS DecryptedSSN;

```

**Explanation of the Code:**

- In this example, the same passphrase 'MySecretPassphrase' used for encryption is defined and stored in the variable `@Passphrase`.

- The previously encrypted SSN data (in VARBINARY format) is stored in the variable `@EncryptedSSN`.

- The DECRYPTBYPASSPHRASE function is used to decrypt the encrypted SSN using the provided passphrase.

- The result is returned as 'DecryptedSSN'.

**Tips:**

- Ensure that you use the same passphrase used for encryption to decrypt the data.

- Protect and manage the passphrase carefully, as it is the key to decrypt the data.

- Be aware of the potential for security risks if the passphrase is compromised, as it can be used to access sensitive data.

- Follow best practices for encryption and key management to maintain data security.

- Be cautious when handling and storing decrypted data, as it may contain sensitive information.
```

4.6 OPENSSL_ENCRYPT

Description:

The OPENSSL_ENCRYPT function in SQL is used to encrypt data using the OpenSSL library. It provides a way to secure data by applying encryption with various encryption algorithms and modes. This function is often used to protect sensitive information stored in a database.

Syntax:

The syntax for the OPENSSL_ENCRYPT function typically includes two parameters:

```sql
OPENSSL_ENCRYPT('encryption_algorithm', 'data_to_encrypt', 'encryption_key'[, 'options'])
```

- "encryption_algorithm": Specifies the encryption algorithm to be used, such as AES-128-CBC, AES-256-GCM, etc.

- "data_to_encrypt": The data you want to encrypt.

- "encryption_key": The key used for encryption. It's important to keep this key secure.

- "options" (Optional): Additional options related to the encryption process.

Example:

Let's take an example where we encrypt a sample text using the AES-128-CBC encryption algorithm:

```sql
```

```
DECLARE @Algorithm NVARCHAR(50) = 'AES-128-CBC';

DECLARE @DataToEncrypt NVARCHAR(100) = 'SensitiveData';

DECLARE @EncryptionKey NVARCHAR(50) = 'MySecretKey';


-- Encrypt data

SELECT OPENSSL_ENCRYPT(@Algorithm, @DataToEncrypt, @EncryptionKey) AS
EncryptedData;
```

Explanation of the Code:

- In this example, we first specify the encryption algorithm (AES-128-CBC), the data to be encrypted ('SensitiveData'), and the encryption key ('MySecretKey').

- The OPENSSL_ENCRYPT function is used to encrypt the data with the specified algorithm and key.

- The result is returned as 'EncryptedData'.

Tips:

- Ensure that you use strong encryption algorithms and modes to enhance data security.

- Protect the encryption key carefully; it's crucial for both encryption and decryption.

- Store the encryption key securely, and consider using hardware security modules (HSMs) for key management.

- Be aware of performance implications, as encryption can be computationally intensive, especially with large datasets.

- Follow best practices for encryption and key management to maintain data security.

4.7 OPENSSL_DECRYPT

Description:

The OPENSSL_DECRYPT function in SQL is used to decrypt data that has been previously encrypted using the OpenSSL library. It is an essential part of securing data by applying decryption to encrypted information. This function is used to access the original data securely, provided you have the correct decryption key.

Syntax:

The syntax for the OPENSSL_DECRYPT function typically includes two parameters:

```sql
OPENSSL_DECRYPT('encryption_algorithm', 'data_to_decrypt', 'decryption_key'[, 'options'])
```

- ``encryption_algorithm``: Specifies the encryption algorithm that was used for encryption, such as AES-128-CBC, AES-256-GCM, etc.

- ``data_to_decrypt``: The encrypted data you want to decrypt.

- ``decryption_key``: The key used for decryption. This key should match the one used for encryption.

- ``options`` (Optional): Additional options related to the decryption process.

Example:

Let's take an example where we decrypt previously encrypted data using the AES-128-CBC encryption algorithm:

```sql
DECLARE @Algorithm NVARCHAR(50) = 'AES-128-CBC';

DECLARE @EncryptedData NVARCHAR(200) = 'EncryptedDataHere';

DECLARE @DecryptionKey NVARCHAR(50) = 'MySecretKey';


-- Decrypt data

SELECT OPENSSL_DECRYPT(@Algorithm, @EncryptedData, @DecryptionKey) AS
DecryptedData;
```

Explanation of the Code:

- In this example, we specify the encryption algorithm (AES-128-CBC), the previously encrypted data ('EncryptedDataHere'), and the decryption key ('MySecretKey').

- The OPENSSL_DECRYPT function is used to decrypt the data with the specified algorithm and key.

- The result is returned as 'DecryptedData'.

Tips:

- Ensure that you use the correct encryption algorithm and decryption key to successfully decrypt the data.

- Keep the decryption key secure and protect it from unauthorized access.

- Encryption and decryption processes should use the same algorithm, mode, and key.

- Maintain strong security practices to safeguard sensitive data during decryption.

- Performance considerations are also important, especially for large datasets, so be aware of potential processing overhead during decryption operations.

- Follow best practices for encryption and key management to maintain data security.

4.8 AES_ENCRYPT

Description:

The AES_ENCRYPT function in SQL is used for encrypting data using the Advanced Encryption Standard (AES) algorithm. AES is a widely used encryption algorithm that provides a high level of security for sensitive data. This function is used to protect data by applying encryption to keep it secure.

Syntax:

The syntax for the AES_ENCRYPT function typically includes two parameters:

```sql
AES_ENCRYPT('data_to_encrypt', 'encryption_key'[, 'options'])
```

- `data_to_encrypt`: Specifies the data you want to encrypt.

- `encryption_key`: The key used for encryption. This key is crucial for both encryption and decryption and should be kept secure.

- `options` (Optional): Additional options related to the encryption process.

Example:

Let's take an example where we encrypt a piece of data using AES encryption:

```sql
DECLARE @DataToEncrypt NVARCHAR(200) = 'SensitiveDataHere';
```

```sql
DECLARE @EncryptionKey NVARCHAR(50) = 'MySecretKey';

-- Encrypt data
SELECT AES_ENCRYPT(@DataToEncrypt, @EncryptionKey) AS EncryptedData;
```

Explanation of the Code:

- In this example, we specify the data to be encrypted ('SensitiveDataHere') and the encryption key ('MySecretKey').

- The AES_ENCRYPT function is used to encrypt the data using the AES algorithm with the provided key.

- The result is returned as 'EncryptedData'.

Tips:

- Ensure that you keep the encryption key secure and protect it from unauthorized access.

- The same encryption key should be used for both encryption and decryption processes.

- AES encryption is a strong encryption method, but its security depends on the strength and secrecy of the encryption key.

- Consider the length and complexity of the encryption key for stronger security.

- Regularly update encryption keys for added security.

- Follow best practices for encryption and key management to maintain data security.

4.9 AES_DECRYPT

Description:

The AES_DECRYPT function in SQL is used for decrypting data that has been previously encrypted using the Advanced Encryption Standard (AES) algorithm. It is the counterpart to AES_ENCRYPT and is used to reverse the encryption process, making the data readable again.

Syntax:

The syntax for the AES_DECRYPT function typically includes two parameters:

```sql
AES_DECRYPT('encrypted_data', 'encryption_key'[, 'options'])
```

- `'encrypted_data'`: Specifies the data that was previously encrypted and needs to be decrypted.

- `'encryption_key'`: The decryption key used for reversing the encryption process. It should be the same key used for encryption.

- `'options'` (Optional): Additional options related to the decryption process.

Example:

Here's an example of how to decrypt data that was previously encrypted using AES encryption:

```sql
DECLARE @EncryptedData VARBINARY(200) = 0x014F89EAAB99D7A...; -- This is the
encrypted data
```

```sql
DECLARE @EncryptionKey NVARCHAR(50) = 'MySecretKey';


-- Decrypt data

SELECT AES_DECRYPT(@EncryptedData, @EncryptionKey) AS DecryptedData;
```

Explanation of the Code:

- In this example, `@EncryptedData` represents the previously encrypted data. Ensure that the data type matches the one you used for encryption.

- `@EncryptionKey` is the same decryption key that was used for encryption.

- The AES_DECRYPT function is used to reverse the encryption process and decrypt the data.

- The result is returned as 'DecryptedData'.

Tips:

- Always use the same encryption key for both encryption and decryption processes. If the keys do not match, decryption will not work.

- Protect the encryption key and keep it secure as it is vital for data protection.

- Regularly update encryption keys to enhance data security.

- Be cautious when handling decrypted data, as it will be in a readable format.

- Always follow security best practices and encryption standards to ensure data security.

4.10 PGP_ENCRYPT

Description:

The PGP_ENCRYPT function in SQL is used for encrypting data using the Pretty Good Privacy (PGP) encryption standard. It is commonly used for encrypting data to ensure its confidentiality and security during storage or transmission. PGP is a widely used method for secure data communication.

Syntax:

The syntax for the PGP_ENCRYPT function typically includes three parameters:

```sql
PGP_ENCRYPT('plain_text', 'public_key', 'options')
```

- `'plain_text'`: Specifies the data that you want to encrypt.

- `'public_key'`: The public key of the recipient, which is used for encryption.

- `'options'` (Optional): Additional options related to the encryption process.

Example:

Here's an example of how to use the PGP_ENCRYPT function to encrypt a message with a recipient's public key:

```sql
DECLARE @PlainText NVARCHAR(200) = 'This is a secret message.';
```

```
DECLARE @PublicKey VARBINARY(2000) = ...; -- Public key of the recipient


-- Encrypt the message with the recipient's public key

DECLARE @EncryptedData VARBINARY(4000);

SET @EncryptedData = PGP_ENCRYPT(@PlainText, @PublicKey);


-- The @EncryptedData variable now contains the encrypted message
```

Explanation of the Code:

- In this example, `@PlainText` contains the message you want to encrypt.

- `@PublicKey` should contain the recipient's public key. Ensure you have the recipient's public key to perform the encryption.

- The PGP_ENCRYPT function is used to encrypt the message using the recipient's public key, and the result is stored in the `@EncryptedData` variable.

Tips:

- Ensure that you have the correct and up-to-date public key of the recipient for successful encryption.

- Keep private keys secure, as they are essential for decrypting PGP-encrypted data.

- Follow PGP best practices for key management, including key revocation and rotation.

- Ensure that both parties (sender and recipient) have the required PGP keys and software to facilitate encryption and decryption.

- PGP encryption is often used for email and file encryption. Understand the specific implementation details and tools used in your environment.

4.11 PGP_DECRYPT

Description:

The PGP_DECRYPT function in SQL is used for decrypting data that has been encrypted using the Pretty Good Privacy (PGP) encryption standard. It is used to recover the original, unencrypted data from PGP-encrypted data. PGP is a widely used method for secure data communication and storage.

Syntax:

The syntax for the PGP_DECRYPT function typically includes two parameters:

```sql
PGP_DECRYPT('encrypted_data', 'private_key')
```

- ``encrypted_data'`: Specifies the PGP-encrypted data that you want to decrypt.

- ``private_key'`: The private key of the recipient or the key associated with the encrypted data.

Example:

Here's an example of how to use the PGP_DECRYPT function to decrypt PGP-encrypted data:

```sql
DECLARE @EncryptedData VARBINARY(4000) = ...; -- PGP-encrypted data

DECLARE @PrivateKey VARBINARY(2000) = ...; -- Private key associated with the
encrypted data
```

```
-- Decrypt the PGP-encrypted data

DECLARE @DecryptedText NVARCHAR(2000);

SET @DecryptedText = PGP_DECRYPT(@EncryptedData, @PrivateKey);


-- The @DecryptedText variable now contains the original message
```

Explanation of the Code:

- In this example, `@EncryptedData` contains the PGP-encrypted data you want to decrypt.

- `@PrivateKey` should contain the private key associated with the encrypted data. The private key is required for decryption.

- The PGP_DECRYPT function is used to decrypt the encrypted data using the private key, and the result is stored in the `@DecryptedText` variable.

Tips:

- Ensure that you have the correct and corresponding private key for the encrypted data to perform successful decryption.

- Keep private keys secure, as they are essential for decrypting PGP-encrypted data.

- Follow PGP best practices for key management, including key revocation and rotation.

- Ensure that both parties (sender and recipient) have the required PGP keys and software to facilitate encryption and decryption.

- PGP encryption is often used for email and file encryption. Understand the specific implementation details and tools used in your environment.

4.12 SHA2

Description:

The SQL SHA2 function is used for computing the SHA-2 (Secure Hash Algorithm 2) hash of a given string or binary data. SHA-2 is a family of cryptographic hash functions designed to provide data integrity and security. These functions generate a fixed-length hash value from the input data, which is typically used to verify the integrity of the data.

Syntax:

The syntax for the SHA2 function typically includes two parameters:

```sql
SHA2(input_string, hash_length)
```

- `input_string`: The string or binary data for which you want to compute the SHA-2 hash.
- `hash_length`: An integer that specifies the length of the hash in bits (either 224, 256, 384, or 512).

Example:

Here's an example of how to use the SHA2 function to compute the SHA-256 hash of a string:

```sql
SELECT SHA2('Hello, World!', 256);
```

Explanation of the Code:

- In this example, the `SHA2` function takes the input string `"Hello, World!"` and computes its SHA-256 hash.

- The second parameter, `256`, indicates that we want to generate a 256-bit hash.

Tips:

- Choose an appropriate hash length based on your security requirements. A longer hash provides greater security but may be slower to compute.

- SHA-2 is widely used for data integrity verification and password storage. Always use it for securely hashing sensitive data.

- Ensure that the input data you provide to SHA2 is in the correct format (string or binary) based on the database system you are using.

- The resulting hash is a fixed-length string of characters and can be stored or transmitted as needed for security purposes.

- When comparing hashed values (e.g., for password verification), always hash the input data in the same way and compare the resulting hashes rather than the original data.

4.13 MD5

Description:

The SQL MD5 function is used for computing the MD5 (Message Digest Algorithm 5) hash of a given string or binary data. MD5 is a widely used cryptographic hash function that produces a 128-bit (16-byte) hash value from the input data. It is commonly used for data integrity verification and password storage.

Syntax:

The syntax for the MD5 function typically includes one parameter:

```sql
MD5(input_string)
```

- `input_string`: The string or binary data for which you want to compute the MD5 hash.

Example:

Here's an example of how to use the MD5 function to compute the MD5 hash of a string:

```sql
SELECT MD5('Hello, World!');
```

Explanation of the Code:

- In this example, the `MD5` function takes the input string "Hello, World!" and computes its MD5 hash.

Tips:

- MD5 is a fast and widely used cryptographic hash function, but it is no longer considered secure for sensitive applications because it is vulnerable to collision attacks. For security-critical applications, consider using more modern hash functions, such as SHA-256 or SHA-3.

- Despite its security limitations, MD5 is still commonly used for non-security-related tasks, such as checksums for data integrity verification.

- Ensure that the input data you provide to MD5 is in the correct format (string or binary) based on the database system you are using.

- The resulting MD5 hash is a fixed-length string of characters (32 characters) and can be stored or transmitted as needed for verification purposes.

- When comparing MD5 hashes (e.g., for data integrity checks), always hash the input data in the same way and compare the resulting hashes rather than the original data.

4.14 SHA1

Description:

The SQL SHA1 function is used to calculate the SHA-1 (Secure Hash Algorithm 1) hash of a given string or binary data. SHA-1 is a cryptographic hash function that produces a 160-bit (20-byte) hash value from the input data. It's often used for data integrity verification, digital signatures, and various security-related applications.

Syntax:

The syntax for the SHA1 function usually includes one parameter:

```sql
SHA1(input_string)
```

- `input_string`: The string or binary data for which you want to compute the SHA-1 hash.

Example:

Here's an example of how to use the SHA1 function to compute the SHA-1 hash of a string:

```sql
SELECT SHA1('Hello, World!');
```

Explanation of the Code:

- In this example, the `SHA1` function takes the input string `"Hello, World!"` and computes its SHA-1 hash.

Tips:

- SHA-1 was once widely used, but it is now considered obsolete for security-sensitive applications due to vulnerabilities like collision attacks. For cryptographic purposes, it's recommended to use more secure hash functions such as SHA-256 or SHA-3.

- Despite its security limitations, SHA-1 is still used in non-security-related tasks such as checksums for data integrity verification.

- Ensure that the input data you provide to SHA1 is in the correct format (string or binary) based on the database system you are using.

- The resulting SHA-1 hash is a fixed-length string of characters (40 characters) and can be stored or transmitted as needed for verification purposes.

- When comparing SHA-1 hashes (e.g., for data integrity checks), always hash the input data in the same way and compare the resulting hashes rather than the original data.

4.15 HMAC

Description:

The SQL HMAC (Hash-based Message Authentication Code) function is used to create a secure hash-based message authentication code for a given message or data using a secret key. HMAC ensures the integrity and authenticity of the message by generating a code that can be verified by the recipient. It is commonly used in secure communication protocols and data authentication.

Syntax:

The syntax for the HMAC function typically includes two parameters:

```sql
HMAC(hash_function, key, message)
```

- `hash_function`: The hash function used to generate the HMAC (e.g., SHA-256, SHA-512).
- `key`: The secret key used for creating the HMAC.
- `message`: The message or data for which you want to create the HMAC.

Example:

Here's an example of how to use the HMAC function with the SHA-256 hash function to create an HMAC for a message:

```sql
```

```
SELECT HMAC('SHA256', 'secret_key', 'Hello, World!');
```

Explanation of the Code:

- In this example, the `HMAC` function is used with the SHA-256 hash function.

- The secret key `'secret_key'` is used to generate the HMAC.

- The HMAC is generated for the message `'Hello, World!'`.

Tips:

- Choose a secure hash function for the HMAC based on your security requirements. Common choices include SHA-256 and SHA-512.

- Keep the secret key confidential, as it is used to verify the authenticity of the message. Do not expose the secret key.

- Verify the HMAC on the recipient's end using the same key and hash function to ensure the integrity of the message.

- HMAC is useful for secure data transfer and authentication, ensuring that data has not been tampered with during transmission.

4.16 PGP_SYM_ENCRYPT

Description:

The SQL `PGP_SYM_ENCRYPT` function is used to encrypt data using the PGP (Pretty Good Privacy) symmetric key encryption algorithm. PGP is a data encryption and decryption program that provides cryptographic privacy and authentication. `PGP_SYM_ENCRYPT` is typically used to encrypt sensitive data for secure storage or transmission, and it uses a passphrase to derive the encryption key.

Syntax:

The syntax for the `PGP_SYM_ENCRYPT` function is as follows:

```sql
PGP_SYM_ENCRYPT(data bytea, passphrase text, options text);
```

- `data`: The data that you want to encrypt, specified as a `bytea` (binary) type.

- `passphrase`: The passphrase or password used to derive the encryption key.

- `options`: Additional encryption options, such as the cipher algorithm and mode.

Example:

Here's an example of how to use `PGP_SYM_ENCRYPT` to encrypt a text message:

```sql
```

```sql
SELECT PGP_SYM_ENCRYPT('Hello, World!', 'my_secret_passphrase', 'cipher-
algo=aes256');
```

Explanation of the Code:

- In this example, the `PGP_SYM_ENCRYPT` function is used to encrypt the text message `"Hello, World!"`.

- The passphrase `"my_secret_passphrase"` is used to derive the encryption key.

- The encryption algorithm `"aes256"` is specified as an option.

Tips:

- Ensure that the passphrase used for encryption is strong and kept secret, as it is used to derive the encryption key.

- Choose appropriate encryption options, such as the cipher algorithm and mode, based on your security requirements.

- PGP symmetric encryption is suitable for encrypting data with a single passphrase for both encryption and decryption.

4.17 PGP_SYM_DECRYPT

Description:

The SQL `PGP_SYM_DECRYPT` function is used to decrypt data that was encrypted using the PGP (Pretty Good Privacy) symmetric key encryption algorithm. PGP is a data encryption and decryption program that provides cryptographic privacy and authentication. `PGP_SYM_DECRYPT` is typically used to decrypt data that was previously encrypted with `PGP_SYM_ENCRYPT` or a similar encryption method. It requires the passphrase that was used for encryption.

Syntax:

The syntax for the `PGP_SYM_DECRYPT` function is as follows:

```sql
PGP_SYM_DECRYPT(data bytea, passphrase text, options text);
```

- `data`: The encrypted data to be decrypted, specified as `bytea` (binary) data.

- `passphrase`: The passphrase or password that was used for encryption and is required for decryption.

- `options`: Additional decryption options, such as the cipher algorithm and mode. These options should match those used during encryption.

Example:

Here's an example of how to use `PGP_SYM_DECRYPT` to decrypt data that was previously encrypted:

```sql
SELECT     PGP_SYM_DECRYPT(encrypted_data,     'my_secret_passphrase',     'cipher-algo=aes256');
```

Explanation of the Code:

- In this example, the `PGP_SYM_DECRYPT` function is used to decrypt `encrypted_data`, which was previously encrypted using the passphrase `'my_secret_passphrase'` and the cipher algorithm `'aes256'`.

- The passphrase used for decryption should match the one used for encryption, and the decryption options must be consistent with the encryption options.

Tips:

- Ensure that you use the correct passphrase for decryption; it should match the passphrase used for encryption.

- Make sure that the decryption options are consistent with the encryption options to successfully decrypt the data.

- PGP symmetric decryption is suitable for decrypting data encrypted with a single passphrase for both encryption and decryption.

4.18 CRYPT

Description:

The SQL `CRYPT` function is used to perform one-way encryption or hashing of data, primarily used for storing passwords securely. It takes a text input and a salt as parameters and returns the encrypted or hashed value of the input. The salt is used to enhance security and generate unique hash values for the same input.

Syntax:

The syntax for the `CRYPT` function is as follows:

```sql
CRYPT(text, salt)
```

- `text`: The text or string to be encrypted or hashed.

- `salt`: A two-character string used as additional input to create a unique hash. The salt should be randomly generated for each piece of data to increase security.

Example:

Here's an example of how to use the `CRYPT` function to hash a password with a random salt:

```sql
SELECT CRYPT('my_password', gen_salt('bf', 8));
```

Explanation of the Code:

- In this example, the `CRYPT` function is used to hash the password `'my_password'` with a random salt generated using the `gen_salt` function. The salt algorithm `'bf'` stands for Blowfish, and the salt size is 8 characters.

- The `CRYPT` function will return a unique hashed value for the given password and salt combination.

Tips:

- The `CRYPT` function is often used for securely storing passwords. When a user logs in, their input password is hashed, and the hash is compared to the stored hash.

- Generate a random salt for each piece of data to ensure that even identical inputs produce different hashes.

- Choose an appropriate salt algorithm and size based on your security requirements. Blowfish (algorithm 'bf') is a commonly used choice.

V.
Mathematical functions

5.1 ABS()

Description:

The SQL `ABS()` function is used to return the absolute (positive) value of a numeric expression. It is commonly used when you want to ensure that a number is positive, regardless of its original sign.

Syntax:

The syntax for the `ABS()` function is as follows:

```sql
ABS(expression)
```

- `expression`: The numeric value or expression for which you want to obtain the absolute value.

Example:

Here's an example of how to use the `ABS()` function:

```sql
SELECT ABS(-5) AS AbsoluteValue;
```

Explanation of the Code:

- In this example, the `ABS()` function is used to calculate the absolute value of -5.

- The result is an absolute value of 5, which is always positive.

Tips:

- The `ABS()` function is useful when you need to work with absolute values, such as in calculations where the sign doesn't matter.

- It can be applied to any numeric data type, including integers and floating-point numbers.

- Be careful when using the `ABS()` function on columns that might contain NULL values. You should handle NULL values appropriately in your SQL query to avoid unexpected results.

5.2 CEIL() / CEILING()

Description:

The SQL `CEIL()` or `CEILING()` function is used to return the smallest integer value that is greater than or equal to a numeric expression. It effectively rounds up a numeric value to the nearest whole number, ensuring that the result is equal to or greater than the original value.

Syntax:

The syntax for the `CEIL()` function or `CEILING()` function is as follows:

```sql
CEIL(expression)
```

or

```sql
CEILING(expression)
```

- `expression`: The numeric value or expression you want to round up.

Example:

Here's an example of how to use the `CEIL()` or `CEILING()` function:

```sql
SELECT CEIL(5.2) AS RoundedUpValue;
```

Explanation of the Code:

- In this example, the `CEIL()` function is used to round up the numeric value 5.2.

- The result is 6, which is the smallest integer value greater than or equal to 5.2.

Tips:

- The `CEIL()` or `CEILING()` function is often used when you need to ensure that a number is rounded up to the nearest integer, regardless of its decimal part.

- Be cautious when using these functions with negative numbers, as they will round up to the nearest whole number, making it less negative or zero if it's close to zero.

- You can use the `FLOOR()` function to round a number down to the nearest integer.

5.3 FLOOR()

Description:

The SQL `FLOOR()` function is used to return the largest integer value that is less than or equal to a numeric expression. It effectively rounds down a numeric value to the nearest whole number, ensuring that the result is equal to or less than the original value.

Syntax:

The syntax for the `FLOOR()` function is as follows:

```sql
FLOOR(expression)
```

- `expression`: The numeric value or expression you want to round down.

Example:

Here's an example of how to use the `FLOOR()` function:

```sql
SELECT FLOOR(5.8) AS RoundedDownValue;
```

Explanation of the Code:

- In this example, the `FLOOR()` function is used to round down the numeric value 5.8.

- The result is 5, which is the largest integer value less than or equal to 5.8.

Tips:

- The `FLOOR()` function is often used when you need to ensure that a number is rounded down to the nearest integer, regardless of its decimal part.

- Be cautious when using this function with negative numbers, as they will round down to the nearest whole number, making it less positive or zero if it's close to zero.

- You can use the `CEIL()` or `CEILING()` function to round a number up to the nearest integer.

5.4 ROUND()

Description:

The SQL `ROUND()` function is used to round a numeric value to a specified number of decimal places or precision. It is commonly used to control the number of decimal places in a value, making it more suitable for presentation or storage purposes.

Syntax:

The syntax for the `ROUND()` function is as follows:

```sql
ROUND(expression, decimals)
```

- `expression`: The numeric value or expression you want to round.
- `decimals`: The number of decimal places to which you want to round the value.

Example:

Here's an example of how to use the `ROUND()` function:

```sql
SELECT ROUND(5.876, 2) AS RoundedValue;
```

Explanation of the Code:

- In this example, the `ROUND()` function is used to round the numeric value 5.876 to two decimal places.

- The result is 5.88, as it has been rounded to two decimal places.

Tips:

- The `ROUND()` function is useful for controlling the precision of numeric values in your SQL queries. It's often used when you want to display values with a specific number of decimal places.

- When rounding, the value is rounded to the nearest value, and if there are two equidistant values, it is rounded to the one with the even digit in the last decimal place. For example, 0.5 is rounded to 0, and 1.5 is rounded to 2.

- If the `decimals` parameter is omitted, `ROUND()` rounds the value to the nearest whole number.

5.5 TRUNCATE()

Description:

The SQL `TRUNCATE()` function is used to remove all decimal places from a numeric value, effectively truncating it to an integer or a number with no decimal part. It can be useful when you want to discard the fractional portion of a number.

Syntax:

The syntax for the `TRUNCATE()` function is as follows:

```sql
TRUNCATE(expression, decimals)
```

- `expression`: The numeric value or expression you want to truncate.
- `decimals`: The number of decimal places to which you want to truncate the value.

Example:

Here's an example of how to use the `TRUNCATE()` function:

```sql
SELECT TRUNCATE(9.875, 1) AS TruncatedValue;
```

Explanation of the Code:

- In this example, the `TRUNCATE()` function is used to remove all decimal places from the numeric value 9.875 to one decimal place.

- The result is 9.8, as the fractional part (0.075) is truncated.

Tips:

- The `TRUNCATE()` function is commonly used when you want to keep only the integer part or a specific number of decimal places from a value.

- Unlike the `ROUND()` function, which rounds the value to the nearest value, `TRUNCATE()` simply removes the decimal portion, which means it always truncates towards zero.

- If the `decimals` parameter is omitted, `TRUNCATE()` removes all decimal places and leaves only the integer part of the number.

5.6 EXP()

Description:

The SQL `EXP()` function is used to calculate the exponential value of a numeric expression. It returns the value of the constant 'e' raised to the power of the specified numeric expression. This function is useful in various mathematical and scientific calculations.

Syntax:

The syntax for the `EXP()` function is as follows:

```sql
EXP(expression)
```

- `expression`: The numeric value or expression for which you want to calculate the exponential value.

Example:

Here's an example of how to use the `EXP()` function:

```sql
SELECT EXP(2) AS ExponentialValue;
```

Explanation of the Code:

- In this example, the `EXP()` function is used to calculate the exponential value of 2.

- The result is approximately 7.389, which is the value of 'e' (Euler's number) raised to the power of 2.

Tips:

- The `EXP()` function is often used in mathematical and scientific calculations, such as compound interest calculations, population growth models, and more.

- 'e' is a mathematical constant approximately equal to 2.71828, and raising 'e' to the power of a value is a fundamental mathematical operation.

- The result of the `EXP()` function is always a positive number, even if the input expression is negative.

5.7 LOG()

Description:

The SQL `LOG()` function is used to calculate the natural logarithm of a numeric expression. It returns the natural logarithm (base 'e') of the specified numeric expression. The natural logarithm is a fundamental mathematical function used in various scientific and mathematical calculations.

Syntax:

The syntax for the `LOG()` function is as follows:

```sql
LOG(expression)
```

- `expression`: The numeric value or expression for which you want to calculate the natural logarithm.

Example:

Here's an example of how to use the `LOG()` function:

```sql
SELECT LOG(10) AS NaturalLogarithm;
```

Explanation of the Code:

- In this example, the `LOG()` function is used to calculate the natural logarithm of 10.

- The result is approximately 2.30259, which is the natural logarithm of 10.

Tips:

- The `LOG()` function is useful in various mathematical and scientific calculations, such as exponential growth and decay, probability calculations, and more.

- The natural logarithm is often denoted as "ln" in mathematical notation.

- The base of the natural logarithm is 'e,' which is approximately equal to 2.71828.

- In SQL, you can calculate logarithms with different bases by using the formula: `LOG(x) / LOG(base)`, where `x` is the numeric expression, and `base` is the desired base of the logarithm.

5.9 POWER() / POW()

Description:

The SQL `POWER()` function is used to raise a number to a specified power. It returns the result of raising a given numeric expression to a specified power. This function is useful when you need to perform exponentiation or calculate values like squared, cubed, etc.

Syntax:

The syntax for the `POWER()` function is as follows:

```sql
POWER(base, exponent)
```

- `base`: The numeric expression or value you want to raise to a power.
- `exponent`: The power to which the base should be raised.

Example:

Here's an example of how to use the `POWER()` function:

```sql
SELECT POWER(2, 3) AS Result;
```

Explanation of the Code:

- In this example, the `POWER()` function calculates 2 raised to the power of 3.

- The result is 8 because 2^3 equals 8.

Tips:

- The `POWER()` function is handy for performing calculations where a number needs to be raised to a specific power. This is especially useful for scientific and mathematical applications.

- The `POW()` function is an alias for `POWER()`, and you can use them interchangeably. Both `POW(2, 3)` and `POWER(2, 3)` would give the same result, 8.

- You can use this function to calculate values such as squares (power of 2), cubes (power of 3), and other exponentiations as needed.

- When dealing with fractional or decimal exponents, the `POWER()` function is very helpful for calculating roots, such as square roots (exponent of 0.5) or cube roots (exponent of 1/3).

5.10 SQRT()

Description:

The SQL `SQRT()` function is used to calculate the square root of a numeric value. It returns the non-negative square root of the specified number. The square root of a number is a value that, when multiplied by itself, equals the original number.

Syntax:

The syntax for the `SQRT()` function is as follows:

```sql
SQRT(number)
```

- `number`: The numeric value for which you want to find the square root.

Example:

Here's an example of how to use the `SQRT()` function:

```sql
SELECT SQRT(25) AS Result;
```

Explanation of the Code:

- In this example, the `SQRT()` function calculates the square root of 25.

- The result is 5 because the square root of 25 is 5 (5 * 5 = 25).

Tips:

- The `SQRT()` function is particularly useful when you need to calculate lengths, distances, or any other value that involves square roots.

- It's essential to provide a non-negative number as the argument to `SQRT()` since square roots of negative numbers are not defined in real numbers.

- Be careful with the data type you provide to the `SQRT()` function. It works with numeric or floating-point data types, so ensure you pass the appropriate data type for accurate results.

5.11 MOD()

Description:

The SQL `MOD()` function, also known as the modulus or modulo function, returns the remainder when one number is divided by another. It is commonly used to find the remainder after performing integer division.

Syntax:

The syntax for the `MOD()` function is as follows:

```sql
MOD(dividend, divisor)
```

- `dividend`: The numeric value that will be divided.
- `divisor`: The numeric value by which the `dividend` is divided.

Example:

Here's an example of how to use the `MOD()` function:

```sql
SELECT MOD(10, 3) AS Remainder;
```

Explanation of the Code:

- In this example, we use the `MOD()` function to find the remainder when 10 is divided by 3.

- The result is 1, because when 10 is divided by 3, it yields a quotient of 3 with a remainder of 1. So, `MOD(10, 3)` returns 1.

Tips:

- The `MOD()` function is particularly useful when you need to perform calculations involving periodicity, cyclic behavior, or determining whether one number is a multiple of another.

- It's important to ensure that the divisor is not zero, as dividing by zero is undefined in mathematics. Be sure to validate the divisor to prevent errors.

- The result of the `MOD()` function will always be between 0 (inclusive) and the absolute value of the divisor (exclusive). In other words, it won't exceed the value of the divisor.

- The `MOD()` function typically works with integers and whole numbers, so it may not provide meaningful results with non-integer data types.

5.12 SIGN()

Description:

The SQL `SIGN()` function is used to determine the sign of a numeric value. It returns one of the following values:

- 1: If the input number is positive.

- 0: If the input number is zero.

- -1: If the input number is negative.

This function is commonly used when you need to categorize numbers based on their sign.

Syntax:

The syntax for the `SIGN()` function is as follows:

```sql
SIGN(number)
```

- `number`: The numeric value for which you want to determine the sign.

Example:

Here's an example of how to use the `SIGN()` function:

```sql
SELECT SIGN(5) AS SignValue;
```

Explanation of the Code:

- In this example, we use the `SIGN()` function to determine the sign of the number 5.

- Since 5 is positive, the `SIGN(5)` function returns 1 as the result.

Tips:

- The `SIGN()` function is useful for categorizing or processing data based on the sign of numeric values. For example, you can use it to classify financial transactions as credits (positive) or debits (negative).

- When using the `SIGN()` function, keep in mind that it's not concerned with the absolute value of the number; it only checks whether the number is positive, zero, or negative.

- The `SIGN()` function can be helpful when building conditional logic or when you need to filter or group records based on the sign of numeric columns.

- The `SIGN()` function typically works with numeric data types, such as integers and floating-point numbers.

5.13 PI()

Description:

The SQL `PI()` function returns the mathematical constant π (pi), which is approximately equal to 3.141592653589793. Pi is a fundamental mathematical constant that represents the ratio of the circumference of a circle to its diameter.

Syntax:

The syntax for the `PI()` function is quite simple as it does not require any arguments:

```sql
PI()
```

Example:

Here's an example of how to use the `PI()` function to retrieve the value of π:

```sql
SELECT PI() AS PiValue;
```

Explanation of the Code:

- In this example, we use the `PI()` function to return the value of π.

- The result will be a single column with the alias `PiValue` and the value approximately equal to 3.141592653589793.

Tips:

- The `PI()` function is a straightforward function that provides the constant value of π. It is often used in mathematical calculations, especially those involving geometry or trigonometry.

- You can use the value of π to calculate various properties of circles and angles in mathematical equations and SQL queries.

- Remember that the value returned by `PI()` is an approximation; for highly precise calculations, you might want to use more decimal places or consider using a specialized mathematical library or software.

- This function is particularly useful in applications such as scientific computing, engineering, and any domain where mathematical constants like π are required.

5.14 RAND()

Description:

The SQL `RAND()` function generates a random decimal number between 0 (inclusive) and 1 (exclusive). It is commonly used for generating random numbers in SQL queries and is helpful for various applications such as simulations, random sampling, or creating test data.

Syntax:

The syntax for the `RAND()` function is simple as it does not require any arguments:

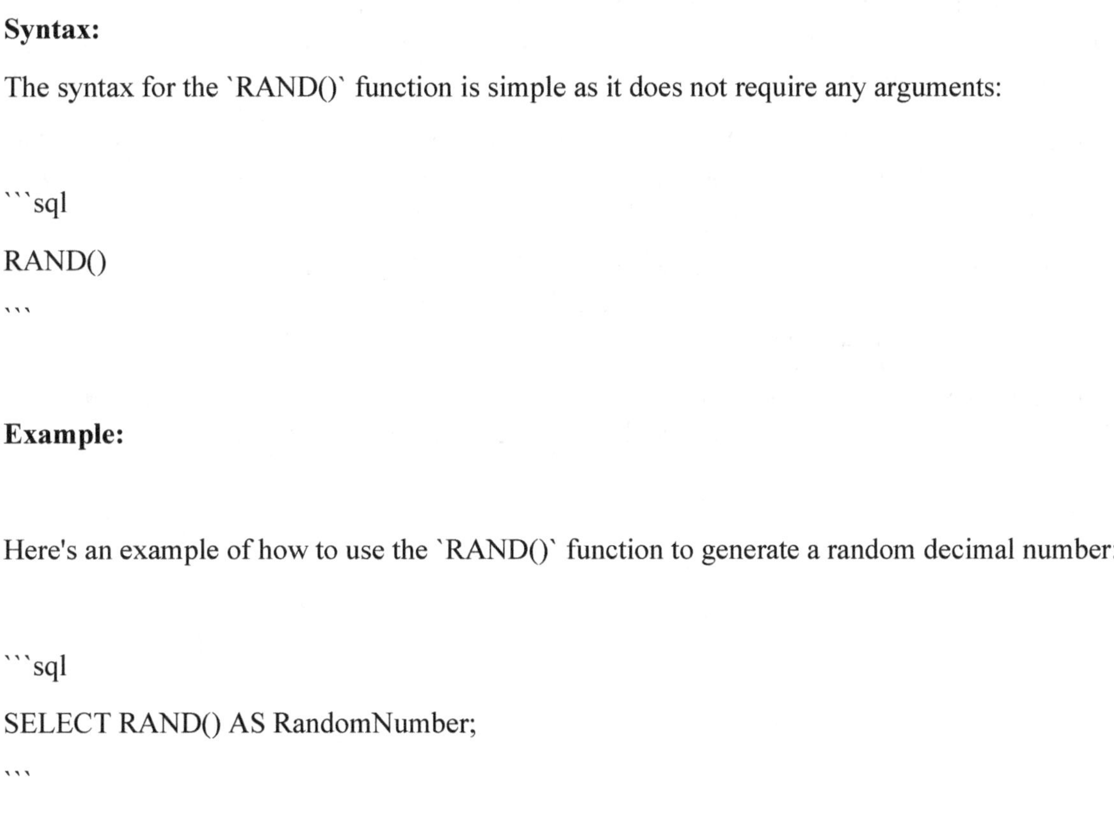

```sql
RAND()
```

Example:

Here's an example of how to use the `RAND()` function to generate a random decimal number:

```sql
SELECT RAND() AS RandomNumber;
```

Explanation of the Code:

- In this example, we use the `RAND()` function to generate a random decimal number between 0 (inclusive) and 1 (exclusive).

- The result will be a single column with the alias `RandomNumber`, containing a random decimal value.

Tips:

- The `RAND()` function generates a pseudo-random number, which means it produces a sequence of numbers that appears random but is determined by an initial value called a seed. If you don't specify a seed, SQL often uses a default seed (e.g., system time), resulting in different sequences each time you run your SQL query.

- To generate a random integer within a specific range, you can use other SQL functions and mathematical operations. For example, you can use `FLOOR(RAND() * (max - min) + min)` to generate random integers between `min` (inclusive) and `max` (exclusive).

- If you want to generate the same sequence of random numbers in subsequent queries, you can set a seed for the `RAND()` function using the `RAND(seed)` form, where `seed` is an integer. This will make the random number sequence repeatable.

- Be cautious when using random numbers in production databases, as the data generated by `RAND()` is not truly random and should not be used for cryptographic or security-related purposes.

5.15 RAND(N)

Description:

The SQL `RAND(N)` function generates a random decimal number between 0 (inclusive) and 1 (exclusive), with the added ability to provide a seed value `N` to make the sequence of random numbers repeatable. It is commonly used for generating random numbers in SQL queries.

Syntax:

The `RAND(N)` function's syntax allows you to specify a seed value `N`, which is optional:

```sql
RAND(N)
```

- `N` (optional): An integer value (seed) used to initialize the random number generator. When `N` is not specified, the generator usually uses a default seed, often based on system time.

Example:

Here's an example of how to use the `RAND(N)` function with a specified seed value:

```sql
SELECT RAND(42) AS RandomNumber;
```

Explanation of the Code:

- In this example, we use the `RAND(42)` function to generate a random decimal number between 0 (inclusive) and 1 (exclusive) with a seed value of 42.

- The result will be a single column with the alias `RandomNumber`, containing a random decimal value. The sequence of random numbers will be the same each time you run the query with a seed of 42.

Tips:

- The `RAND(N)` function allows you to set a specific seed value, which makes the sequence of random numbers repeatable. When you use the same seed, you'll get the same sequence of random numbers.

- Be cautious when using random numbers in production databases, as the data generated by `RAND()` is not truly random and should not be used for cryptographic or security-related purposes.

- If you don't specify a seed (i.e., use `RAND()` without an argument), SQL often uses a default seed, typically based on system time, resulting in different sequences each time you run your SQL query.

- To generate random integers within a specific range, you can use other SQL functions and mathematical operations. For example, you can use `FLOOR(RAND(42) * (max - min) + min)` to generate random integers between `min` (inclusive) and `max` (exclusive) with a repeatable sequence.

5.16 ACOS()

Description:

The SQL `ACOS()` function, short for "Arc Cosine," is used to calculate the arccosine of a specified numeric expression, returning the angle in radians. It is a trigonometric function commonly used to find the angle (in radians) whose cosine is the given value. This function can be helpful in various applications, such as calculating angles in geometry or physics.

Syntax:

The `ACOS()` function's syntax is straightforward. You provide a numeric expression as an argument:

```sql
ACOS(numeric_expression)
```

- `numeric_expression`: A number or numeric expression for which you want to find the arccosine. The expression should be within the range of -1 to 1.

Example:

Here's an example of how to use the `ACOS()` function in SQL:

```sql
SELECT ACOS(0.5) AS ArcCosineValue;
```

```
```

Explanation of the Code:

- In this example, we use the `ACOS(0.5)` function to calculate the arccosine of 0.5.

- The result will be a single column with the alias `ArcCosineValue`, containing the angle in radians whose cosine is 0.5.

Tips:

- The input to the `ACOS()` function should be a numeric expression within the range of -1 to 1. Attempting to use values outside this range will result in an error.

- The `ACOS()` function returns an angle in radians. If you need the result in degrees, you can convert it by multiplying the result by `(180 / PI())`, where `PI()` is a built-in SQL function that returns the value of π (pi).

- Be cautious when using trigonometric functions like `ACOS()` in SQL, as they can significantly affect query performance, especially when used on large datasets.

5.17 ASIN()

Description:

The SQL `ASIN()` function, short for "Arc Sine," is used to calculate the arcsine of a specified numeric expression, returning the angle in radians. It is a trigonometric function commonly used to find the angle (in radians) whose sine is the given value. This function is useful in various applications, such as calculating angles in geometry or physics.

Syntax:

The `ASIN()` function's syntax is straightforward. You provide a numeric expression as an argument:

```sql
ASIN(numeric_expression)
```

- `numeric_expression`: A number or numeric expression for which you want to find the arcsine. The expression should be within the range of -1 to 1.

Example:

Here's an example of how to use the `ASIN()` function in SQL:

```sql
SELECT ASIN(0.7071) AS ArcSineValue;
```

```
```

Explanation of the Code:

- In this example, we use the `ASIN(0.7071)` function to calculate the arcsine of 0.7071.

- The result will be a single column with the alias `ArcSineValue`, containing the angle in radians whose sine is 0.7071.

Tips:

- The input to the `ASIN()` function should be a numeric expression within the range of -1 to 1. Attempting to use values outside this range will result in an error.

- The `ASIN()` function returns an angle in radians. If you need the result in degrees, you can convert it by multiplying the result by `(180 / PI())`, where `PI()` is a built-in SQL function that returns the value of π (pi).

- Be cautious when using trigonometric functions like `ASIN()` in SQL, as they can significantly affect query performance, especially when used on large datasets.

5.18 ATAN()

Description:

The SQL `ATAN()` function, short for "Arc Tangent," is used to calculate the arctangent of a specified numeric expression, returning the angle in radians. It is a trigonometric function commonly used to find the angle (in radians) whose tangent is the given value. This function is useful in various applications, such as calculating angles in geometry or physics.

Syntax:

The `ATAN()` function's syntax is straightforward. You provide a numeric expression as an argument:

```sql
ATAN(numeric_expression)
```

- `numeric_expression`: A number or numeric expression for which you want to find the arctangent.

Example:

Here's an example of how to use the `ATAN()` function in SQL:

```sql
SELECT ATAN(1) AS ArcTangentValue;
```

```
```

Explanation of the Code:

- In this example, we use the `ATAN(1)` function to calculate the arctangent of 1.

- The result will be a single column with the alias `ArcTangentValue`, containing the angle in radians whose tangent is 1.

Tips:

- The `ATAN()` function returns an angle in radians. If you need the result in degrees, you can convert it by multiplying the result by `(180 / PI())`, where `PI()` is a built-in SQL function that returns the value of π (pi).

- Be cautious when using trigonometric functions like `ATAN()` in SQL, as they can significantly affect query performance, especially when used on large datasets.

- Remember that the result of `ATAN(1)` is $\pi/4$ radians or 45 degrees.

5.19 ATAN2()

Description:

The SQL `ATAN2()` function, short for "Arc Tangent 2," is used to calculate the arctangent of the quotient of two specified numeric expressions. It returns the angle in radians. The `ATAN2()` function is a variation of the `ATAN()` function and is useful when you need to calculate the arctangent of the ratio of two numbers, typically representing coordinates in the Cartesian plane.

Syntax:

The `ATAN2()` function's syntax requires two numeric expressions as arguments:

```sql
ATAN2(numeric_expression1, numeric_expression2)
```

- `numeric_expression1`: The numerator, which represents the vertical position or change in the Cartesian plane.

- `numeric_expression2`: The denominator, which represents the horizontal position or change in the Cartesian plane.

Example:

Here's an example of how to use the `ATAN2()` function in SQL:

```sql
```

```
SELECT ATAN2(2, 1) AS ArcTangentValue;
```

Explanation of the Code:

- In this example, we use the `ATAN2(2, 1)` function to calculate the arctangent of the ratio of 2 to 1, which corresponds to a point with coordinates (1,2) in the Cartesian plane.

- The result will be a single column with the alias `ArcTangentValue`, containing the angle in radians whose tangent is the ratio of 2 to 1.

Tips:

- The `ATAN2()` function is particularly useful in scenarios where you need to calculate angles or directions based on coordinate differences, such as in geometry or navigation applications.

- The result of `ATAN2()` is in radians. If you need the result in degrees, you can convert it by multiplying the result by `(180 / PI())`, where `PI()` is a built-in SQL function that returns the value of π (pi).

- Like the `ATAN()` function, be mindful of performance when using `ATAN2()` on large datasets, as trigonometric functions can be computationally expensive.

5.20 COS()

Description:

The SQL `COS()` function, short for "Cosine," is used to calculate the cosine of an angle specified in radians. It's one of the trigonometric functions and is often used in geometry, physics, and engineering for various calculations involving angles and circular motion.

Syntax:

The `COS()` function in SQL has a straightforward syntax. You provide the angle in radians as the argument, and it returns the cosine value.

```sql
COS(angle_in_radians)
```

- `angle_in_radians`: The angle in radians for which you want to calculate the cosine value.

Example:

Here's an example of how to use the `COS()` function in SQL:

```sql
SELECT COS(0) AS CosineValue;
```

Explanation of the Code:

- In this example, we use the `COS(0)` function to calculate the cosine of 0 radians. The cosine of 0 is 1, which means that the angle is 0 degrees, or a full circle.

Tips:

- Ensure that you provide the `COS()` function with an angle in radians. If you have an angle in degrees, you'll need to convert it to radians first. The conversion formula is `(angle_in_radians = angle_in_degrees * π / 180)`. You can use the `PI()` function to get the value of π.

- The `COS()` function can be used for various applications, such as calculating distances, positions, and oscillations in physics, as well as angles and rotations in computer graphics and gaming.

- When working with SQL databases, be aware of the input units (radians or degrees) and whether your database system provides a built-in conversion function if you need to switch between these units.

- Trigonometric functions like `COS()` can be computationally expensive, so use them thoughtfully on large datasets or in performance-critical applications.

5.21 SIN()

Description:

The SQL `SIN()` function, short for "Sine," is used to calculate the sine of an angle specified in radians. It's one of the trigonometric functions and is often used in geometry, physics, and engineering for various calculations involving angles and circular motion.

Syntax:

The `SIN()` function in SQL has a straightforward syntax. You provide the angle in radians as the argument, and it returns the sine value.

```sql
SIN(angle_in_radians)
```

- `angle_in_radians`: The angle in radians for which you want to calculate the sine value.

Example:

Here's an example of how to use the `SIN()` function in SQL:

```sql
SELECT SIN(0) AS SineValue;
```

Explanation of the Code:

- In this example, we use the `SIN(0)` function to calculate the sine of 0 radians. The sine of 0 is 0, which means that the angle is 0 degrees, or a full circle.

Tips:

- Ensure that you provide the `SIN()` function with an angle in radians. If you have an angle in degrees, you'll need to convert it to radians first. The conversion formula is `(angle_in_radians = angle_in_degrees * π / 180)`. You can use the `PI()` function to get the value of π.

- The `SIN()` function can be used for various applications, such as calculating distances, positions, and oscillations in physics, as well as angles and rotations in computer graphics and gaming.

- When working with SQL databases, be aware of the input units (radians or degrees) and whether your database system provides a built-in conversion function if you need to switch between these units.

- Trigonometric functions like `SIN()` can be computationally expensive, so use them thoughtfully on large datasets or in performance-critical applications.

5.22 TAN()

Description:

The SQL `TAN()` function, short for "Tangent," is a trigonometric function used to calculate the tangent of an angle specified in radians. The tangent is a ratio of the length of the side opposite the angle to the length of the side adjacent to the angle in a right triangle. The `TAN()` function is used in geometry, physics, and engineering for various calculations involving angles.

Syntax:

The `TAN()` function in SQL has a straightforward syntax. You provide the angle in radians as the argument, and it returns the tangent value.

```sql
TAN(angle_in_radians)
```

- `angle_in_radians`: The angle in radians for which you want to calculate the tangent value.

Example:

Here's an example of how to use the `TAN()` function in SQL:

```sql
SELECT TAN(1) AS TangentValue;
```

Explanation of the Code:

- In this example, we use the `TAN(1)` function to calculate the tangent of 1 radian. The result is approximately 1.5574077246549023. This means that in a right triangle, the length of the side opposite the angle of 1 radian is about 1.5574 times the length of the side adjacent to the angle.

Tips:

- Ensure that you provide the `TAN()` function with an angle in radians. If you have an angle in degrees, you'll need to convert it to radians first. The conversion formula is `(angle_in_radians = angle_in_degrees * π / 180)`. You can use the `PI()` function to get the value of π.

- The tangent is undefined for certain values, such as multiples of 90 degrees (or $\pi/2$ radians), because the length of the side adjacent to the angle is 0. So, be cautious when using `TAN()` for angles near these values.

- The `TAN()` function can be used in various applications, including calculating slopes, inclinations, and angular relationships in various fields.

- Trigonometric functions like `TAN()` can be computationally expensive, so use them thoughtfully on large datasets or in performance-critical applications.

5.23 DEGREES()

Description:

The SQL `DEGREES()` function is used to convert an angle from radians to degrees. In trigonometry, angles can be measured in both radians and degrees, and this function allows you to switch between these two units of angular measurement.

Syntax:

The `DEGREES()` function in SQL has a simple syntax. You provide the angle in radians as the argument, and it returns the equivalent angle in degrees.

```sql
DEGREES(angle_in_radians)
```

- `angle_in_radians`: The angle in radians that you want to convert to degrees.

Example:

Here's an example of how to use the `DEGREES()` function in SQL:

```sql
SELECT DEGREES(1.0471975511965979) AS DegreesValue;
```

Explanation of the Code:

- In this example, we use the `DEGREES(1.0471975511965979)` function to convert an angle of approximately 1.047 radians to degrees. The result is approximately 60 degrees. This means that an angle of 1.047 radians is equivalent to 60 degrees.

Tips:

- The `DEGREES()` function is especially useful when you're working with trigonometric calculations in SQL and need to present the results in degrees instead of radians.

- Ensure that you provide the `DEGREES()` function with an angle in radians. If you have an angle in degrees and want to convert it to radians, you can use the `RADIANS()` function.

- The conversion formula from radians to degrees is: `angle_in_degrees = angle_in_radians * 180 / π`, where π (pi) is a mathematical constant (approximately 3.141592653589793).

- When dealing with angles in SQL, make sure to be consistent with your units (radians or degrees) to avoid errors in your calculations.

- Consider using this function when working with spatial data, geometry, or any domain where angles are expressed in different units.

5.24 RADIANS()

Description:

The SQL `RADIANS()` function is used to convert an angle from degrees to radians. In trigonometry, angles can be measured in both degrees and radians, and this function allows you to switch between these two units of angular measurement.

Syntax:

The `RADIANS()` function in SQL has a simple syntax. You provide the angle in degrees as the argument, and it returns the equivalent angle in radians.

```sql
RADIANS(angle_in_degrees)
```

- `angle_in_degrees`: The angle in degrees that you want to convert to radians.

Example:

Here's an example of how to use the `RADIANS()` function in SQL:

```sql
SELECT RADIANS(90) AS RadiansValue;
```

Explanation of the Code:

- In this example, we use the `RADIANS(90)` function to convert an angle of 90 degrees to radians. The result is approximately 1.5707963267948966 radians. This means that an angle of 90 degrees is equivalent to approximately 1.5708 radians.

Tips:

- The `RADIANS()` function is especially useful when you're working with trigonometric calculations in SQL and need to present the results in radians instead of degrees.

- Ensure that you provide the `RADIANS()` function with an angle in degrees. If you have an angle in radians and want to convert it to degrees, you can use the `DEGREES()` function.

- The conversion formula from degrees to radians is: `angle_in_radians = angle_in_degrees * π / 180`, where π (pi) is a mathematical constant (approximately 3.141592653589793).

- When dealing with angles in SQL, make sure to be consistent with your units (radians or degrees) to avoid errors in your calculations.

- Consider using this function when working with spatial data, geometry, or any domain where angles are expressed in different units.

VI.
Logical functions and Operators

6.1 AND

Description:

The SQL `AND` operator is a logical operator used to combine two or more Boolean conditions. It returns `TRUE` if all the conditions are true, and `FALSE` if at least one of the conditions is false. The `AND` operator allows you to perform logical conjunction in SQL queries, which means that all the conditions must be true for the result to be true.

Syntax:

The `AND` operator in SQL is used to combine two or more conditions in the `WHERE` clause of a `SELECT`, `UPDATE`, or `DELETE` statement.

```sql
condition1 AND condition2
```

- `condition1`, `condition2`, ...: Boolean expressions that you want to combine. These can be simple comparisons, complex expressions, or other logical conditions.

Example:

Here's an example of how to use the `AND` operator in SQL:

Suppose you have a table named `Products` and you want to retrieve all products with a price between $10 and $50 and with a stock quantity greater than 100.

```sql
SELECT * FROM Products

WHERE Price >= 10 AND Price <= 50 AND StockQuantity > 100;
```

Explanation of the Code:

- In this example, we use the `AND` operator to combine three conditions in the `WHERE` clause. These conditions are:

  1. `Price >= 10`: Selects products with a price greater than or equal to $10.

  2. `Price <= 50`: Selects products with a price less than or equal to $50.

  3. `StockQuantity > 100`: Selects products with a stock quantity greater than 100.

- The result is a list of products that meet all three conditions.

Tips:

- The `AND` operator is often used in combination with other logical operators like `OR` to create more complex conditions.

- Ensure that you use parentheses to control the order of evaluation when combining multiple conditions. For example, `(A AND B) OR C` might produce a different result than `A AND (B OR C)` depending on your intended logic.

- Be cautious when using the `AND` operator with large datasets because it can impact query performance. Consider optimizing your queries and indexing your database if necessary.

- Use comments in your SQL queries to make the logic of complex conditions clear to other developers and for future reference.

6.2 OR

Description:

The SQL `OR` operator is a logical operator used to combine two or more Boolean conditions. It returns `TRUE` if at least one of the conditions is true, and `FALSE` only if all the conditions are false. The `OR` operator allows you to perform logical disjunction in SQL queries, which means that any one of the conditions must be true for the result to be true.

Syntax:

The `OR` operator in SQL is used to combine two or more conditions in the `WHERE` clause of a `SELECT`, `UPDATE`, or `DELETE` statement.

```sql
condition1 OR condition2
```

- `condition1`, `condition2`, ...: Boolean expressions that you want to combine. These can be simple comparisons, complex expressions, or other logical conditions.

Example:

Here's an example of how to use the `OR` operator in SQL:

Suppose you have a table named `Employees` and you want to retrieve all employees who are either in the "Sales" department or have a salary greater than $60,000.

```sql
SELECT * FROM Employees

WHERE Department = 'Sales' OR Salary > 60000;
```

Explanation of the Code:

- In this example, we use the `OR` operator to combine two conditions in the `WHERE` clause. These conditions are:

  1. `Department = 'Sales'`: Selects employees in the "Sales" department.

  2. `Salary > 60000`: Selects employees with a salary greater than $60,000.

- The result is a list of employees who meet either of these conditions.

Tips:

- The `OR` operator is often used in combination with other logical operators like `AND` to create more complex conditions.

- Ensure that you use parentheses to control the order of evaluation when combining multiple conditions. For example, `(A OR B) AND C` might produce a different result than `A OR (B AND C)` depending on your intended logic.

- Be cautious when using the `OR` operator with large datasets because it can impact query performance. Consider optimizing your queries and indexing your database if necessary.

- Use comments in your SQL queries to make the logic of complex conditions clear to other developers and for future reference.

6.3 NOT

Description:

The SQL `NOT` operator is a logical operator used to reverse the value of a Boolean expression. It returns `TRUE` if the expression is `FALSE`, and `FALSE` if the expression is `TRUE`. In essence, it negates or flips the result of a Boolean condition. The `NOT` operator is a fundamental component of SQL for creating negative conditions or filtering rows that do not meet a certain criterion.

Syntax:

The `NOT` operator is used to negate a Boolean expression.

```sql
NOT condition
```

- `condition`: The Boolean expression or condition that you want to negate.

Example:

Here's an example of how to use the `NOT` operator in SQL:

Suppose you have a table named `Products` and you want to retrieve all products that are not in the "Discontinued" status.

```sql
SELECT * FROM Products

WHERE NOT Status = 'Discontinued';
```

Explanation of the Code:

- In this example, we use the `NOT` operator to negate the condition `Status = 'Discontinued'`. This condition selects products with a status other than "Discontinued."

- The result is a list of products that are currently available or have a status other than "Discontinued."

Tips:

- The `NOT` operator is often used in combination with other logical operators like `AND` and `OR` to create complex conditions and to filter rows based on negative criteria.

- It's essential to understand the order of evaluation when using `NOT` in conjunction with other operators. Using parentheses to control the order of operations is a good practice.

- The `NOT` operator can be used for filtering, checking for the absence of specific values, or ensuring that a column's value doesn't match a certain condition.

- Make your queries and conditions more readable by using comments, especially in complex SQL statements that involve negations. This helps other developers and your future self understand the logic.

6.4 IF / ELSE

Description:

The SQL `IF` and `ELSE` statements are used for conditional execution of code blocks within a SQL query or stored procedure. They allow you to perform different actions based on a specified condition. These statements are particularly useful for making decisions or implementing branching logic in your SQL code.

Syntax:

The `IF` statement typically has the following syntax:

```sql
IF condition

   BEGIN

      -- Code to execute if the condition is true

   END
ELSE

   BEGIN

      -- Code to execute if the condition is false

   END
```

- `condition`: The Boolean expression or condition you want to test.

Example:

Here's an example of how to use the `IF` and `ELSE` statements in SQL:

Suppose you want to retrieve information about a customer based on their loyalty level:

```sql
DECLARE @LoyaltyLevel INT = 2;

IF @LoyaltyLevel = 1
  BEGIN
    PRINT 'Basic Member';
  END
ELSE IF @LoyaltyLevel = 2
  BEGIN
    PRINT 'Silver Member';
  END
ELSE IF @LoyaltyLevel = 3
  BEGIN
    PRINT 'Gold Member';
  END
ELSE
  BEGIN
```

```
    PRINT 'Not a Member';

  END

```

Explanation of the Code:

- In this example, we declare a variable `@LoyaltyLevel` with a value of `2`.

- The `IF` and `ELSE IF` statements are used to check the value of `@LoyaltyLevel` and determine the customer's loyalty level.

- The code block following each `IF` statement specifies the action to take if the condition is true.

Tips:

- SQL `IF` and `ELSE` statements are often used in stored procedures, functions, and dynamic SQL queries to add conditional behavior.

- Use proper indentation and formatting to make your SQL code more readable.

- Be cautious when nesting `IF` and `ELSE` statements, as it can quickly become complex. Try to keep your conditional logic as simple as possible.

- You can also use `CASE` expressions for conditional logic in SQL, especially when the logic involves a single value to be computed based on multiple conditions.

- Avoid using `IF` and `ELSE` statements for complex data manipulation; they are more suitable for controlling the flow of your SQL code based on simple conditions.

6.5 CASE

Description:

The SQL `CASE` expression is used for conditional logic within a SQL query or a stored procedure. It allows you to perform different actions based on a specified condition or set of conditions. The `CASE` expression is particularly useful for making decisions, creating calculated fields, or applying conditional logic to the result set of a query.

Syntax:

The `CASE` expression has two main formats: simple and searched.

1. Simple `CASE` expression:

```sql
CASE expression
    WHEN value1 THEN result1
    WHEN value2 THEN result2
    -- Additional WHEN clauses
    ELSE else_result
END
```

- `expression`: The value to be compared.

- `value1`, `value2`, etc.: The values to compare `expression` to.

- `result1`, `result2`, etc.: The result to return if `expression` matches the corresponding `value`.

- `else_result`: The result to return if no matches are found.

2. Searched `CASE` expression:

```sql
CASE
    WHEN condition1 THEN result1
    WHEN condition2 THEN result2
    -- Additional WHEN clauses
    ELSE else_result
END
```

- `condition1`, `condition2`, etc.: The conditions to be evaluated.
- `result1`, `result2`, etc.: The result to return if the corresponding condition is true.
- `else_result`: The result to return if no conditions are true.

Examples:

Here are examples of how to use the `CASE` expression in SQL:

1. Simple `CASE` expression:

Suppose you want to categorize products into three price ranges (Low, Medium, High) based on their prices:

```sql
SELECT ProductName, Price,
  CASE
    WHEN Price < 50 THEN 'Low'
    WHEN Price <= 100 THEN 'Medium'
    ELSE 'High'
  END AS PriceRange
FROM Products;
```

In this example, the `CASE` expression checks the price of each product and assigns it a price range based on the conditions.

2. Searched `CASE` expression:

Suppose you want to categorize students into different grade categories based on their exam scores:

```sql
SELECT StudentName, ExamScore,
  CASE
    WHEN ExamScore >= 90 THEN 'A'
    WHEN ExamScore >= 80 THEN 'B'
```

```
        WHEN ExamScore >= 70 THEN 'C'

        WHEN ExamScore >= 60 THEN 'D'

        ELSE 'F'

    END AS Grade

FROM Students;

```

In this example, the `CASE` expression evaluates each student's exam score and assigns a grade based on the conditions.

Explanation of the Code:

- In the first example, the `CASE` expression is used to categorize products into three price ranges based on the specified conditions.

- In the second example, the `CASE` expression is used to assign grades to students based on their exam scores.

Tips:

- The `CASE` expression is a versatile tool for adding conditional logic to your SQL queries. It can be used in `SELECT` statements, `WHERE` clauses, and other parts of SQL queries.

- You can use multiple `WHEN` clauses to handle different conditions.

- Ensure that you provide a sensible `ELSE` clause to handle cases where none of the conditions are met.

- Be consistent with formatting and indentation to make your SQL code more readable.

- Consider using `CASE` expressions in combination with aggregate functions or window functions to calculate derived fields or perform conditional aggregations.

- The `CASE` expression is often a more elegant and efficient way to express conditional logic than using multiple `IF` or `ELSE IF` statements.

6.6 COALESCE

Description:

The SQL `COALESCE` function is used to return the first non-null expression in a list of expressions. It's particularly useful when you need to handle potential NULL values in your SQL queries and return a meaningful result.

Syntax:

```sql
COALESCE(expression1, expression2, expression3, ...)
```

- `expression1`, `expression2`, `expression3`, etc.: A list of expressions that you want to evaluate in order. The function returns the value of the first expression that is not `NULL`.

Example:

Suppose you have a table of orders with an optional discount percentage, and you want to calculate the actual price for each order. If a discount percentage is provided, it should be applied; otherwise, the full price should be used.

```sql
SELECT OrderID, OrderDate, TotalPrice,
    COALESCE(DiscountPercentage, 0) AS AppliedDiscount,
```

```
    TotalPrice - (TotalPrice * COALESCE(DiscountPercentage, 0) / 100) AS FinalPrice
FROM Orders;
```

In this example, the `COALESCE` function is used to handle the potential `NULL` value for the `DiscountPercentage` column. If there's a discount percentage, it's applied, and if the column is `NULL`, a default value of 0 is used. The `FinalPrice` is then calculated based on the applied discount.

Explanation of the Code:

- The SQL query selects data from an `Orders` table, including the order ID, order date, total price, and discount percentage.

- The `COALESCE` function is used to handle the potential `NULL` value in the `DiscountPercentage` column. If `DiscountPercentage` is not `NULL`, it's used. If it is `NULL`, a default value of 0 is used.

- The `AppliedDiscount` column stores the applied discount (either the original value or 0 if `NULL`).

- The `FinalPrice` is calculated by subtracting the discount amount from the `TotalPrice` when a discount is applied.

Tips:

- `COALESCE` is commonly used to provide default values for columns that may contain `NULL` values, ensuring that calculations or comparisons won't fail.

- You can use multiple expressions within `COALESCE`. The function returns the first non-`NULL` value in the list. For example, `COALESCE(expression1, expression2, expression3)` returns the first non-`NULL` value among the three expressions.

- `COALESCE` is a SQL-standard function supported by various relational database management systems, including MySQL, PostgreSQL, SQL Server, Oracle, and others.

- Be cautious when using `COALESCE` for numeric columns; ensure the default value is of the correct data type to avoid unexpected data type conversions.

- Use `COALESCE` within `SELECT` statements, `WHERE` clauses, and expressions where you need to handle potential `NULL` values effectively.

- Other similar functions, such as `ISNULL` in SQL Server or `NVL` in Oracle, provide similar functionality, but `COALESCE` is a more generic SQL standard function.

6.7 IN

Description:

The SQL `IN` operator is used to filter query results based on a specified list of values. It allows you to specify a condition in which a column's value should match any value from a list.

Syntax:

```sql
SELECT column1, column2, ...
FROM table_name
WHERE column_name IN (value1, value2, ...);
```

- `column1`, `column2`, ...: The columns you want to retrieve.
- `table_name`: The table from which to select data.
- `column_name`: The column you want to filter.
- `value1`, `value2`, ...: The list of values to compare against the specified column.

Example:

Suppose you have a `Products` table, and you want to select products with specific product IDs.

```sql
```

```
SELECT ProductName, Price

FROM Products

WHERE ProductID IN (101, 103, 105);
```

In this example, the `IN` operator is used to filter products based on their product IDs. The query will return the product name and price for products with IDs 101, 103, and 105.

Explanation of the Code:

- The SQL query selects data from the `Products` table, specifically the `ProductName` and `Price` columns.

- The `WHERE` clause filters the results. The `ProductID` column is checked against the values specified in the `IN` clause: 101, 103, and 105.

- The query returns only the rows where the `ProductID` matches any of the specified values.

Tips:

- The `IN` operator is used to simplify the filtering of data when you have multiple possible values that a column might match.

- You can use the `IN` operator with text, numeric, or date values.

- You can also use subqueries with the `IN` operator to dynamically retrieve a list of values to compare against a column.

- When specifying values in the `IN` clause, make sure the data types match the column you're comparing with to avoid unexpected results.

- Use the `NOT IN` operator to filter rows where a column's value does not match any value in the specified list.

- Consider using the `IN` operator within the `WHERE` clause of `SELECT`, `UPDATE`, or `DELETE` statements.

- The `IN` operator can be an efficient alternative to multiple `OR` conditions when you need to check for equality against multiple values.

- Ensure that the list of values in the `IN` clause is enclosed in parentheses.

6.8 LIKE

Description:

The SQL `LIKE` operator is used to search for a specified pattern in a column. It is often used with wildcard characters to match patterns within text or string data.

Syntax:

```sql
SELECT column1, column2, ...
FROM table_name
WHERE column_name LIKE pattern;
```

- `column1`, `column2`, ...: The columns you want to retrieve.
- `table_name`: The table from which to select data.
- `column_name`: The column you want to search for a pattern.
- `pattern`: The pattern you want to search for, which can include wildcard characters.

Wildcard Characters:

- `%`: Represents zero or more characters.
- `_`: Represents a single character.

Example:

Suppose you have a `Customers` table, and you want to select customers whose names start with "A."

```sql
SELECT CustomerName

FROM Customers

WHERE CustomerName LIKE 'A%';
```

In this example, the `LIKE` operator is used to filter customers whose names begin with the letter "A."

Explanation of the Code:

- The SQL query selects data from the `Customers` table, specifically the `CustomerName` column.

- The `WHERE` clause filters the results. The `CustomerName` column is checked using the `LIKE` operator with the pattern `'A%'`. This means it will match any name that starts with "A."

- The query returns a list of customer names that satisfy the pattern condition.

Tips:

- The `LIKE` operator is used for pattern matching with text or string data.

- The `%` wildcard character can be used to match any sequence of characters (including none), while the `_` wildcard character matches a single character.

- You can use `%` at the beginning, end, or in the middle of a pattern to match various patterns. For example, `"A%"` matches names starting with "A," `"%a"` matches names ending with "a," and `"%or%"` matches names containing "or."

- The `LIKE` operator is often used with `SELECT` statements to filter rows based on patterns.

- To match names that start with a single character and have at least three more characters following it, you can use the pattern `"_%_%_%"`.

- When working with case-sensitive data, use the `COLLATE` clause to specify a case-insensitive collation (e.g., `COLLATE Latin1_General_CI_AS`) within the `LIKE` operator.

- You can combine wildcard characters in various ways to create more complex patterns for matching.

- Use square brackets `[]` to match any single character from a specified set of characters (e.g., `"M[ae]tch"` matches "Match" and "Metch").

6.9 BETWEEN

Description:

The SQL `BETWEEN` operator is used to filter the result set within a specific range of values. It allows you to select values that are within a given range, inclusive of the endpoints.

Syntax:

```sql
SELECT column1, column2, ...
FROM table_name
WHERE column_name BETWEEN value1 AND value2;
```

- `column1`, `column2`, ...: The columns you want to retrieve.

- `table_name`: The table from which to select data.

- `column_name`: The column you want to apply the range filter to.

- `value1` and `value2`: The range of values you want to filter.

Example:

Let's say you have a `Products` table and you want to select products with prices between $10 and $50.

```sql
SELECT ProductName, Price

FROM Products

WHERE Price BETWEEN 10 AND 50;
```

Explanation of the Code:

- The SQL query selects data from the `Products` table, specifically the `ProductName` and `Price` columns.

- The `WHERE` clause filters the results. The `Price` column is checked using the `BETWEEN` operator with the range from 10 to 50. This means it selects products with prices between $10 and $50, inclusive of those values.

- The query returns a list of product names and their corresponding prices that satisfy the range condition.

Tips:

- The `BETWEEN` operator checks if a value lies within a specified range and includes the endpoints.

- The range values can be numbers, dates, or text, depending on the data type of the column.

- Ensure that the data type of the column and the data type of the values in the range are compatible.

- You can use `NOT BETWEEN` to select values outside of the specified range.

- Be cautious with date and time ranges, as the time portion might affect the inclusiveness of the range.

- When filtering on text columns, be aware of case sensitivity and any leading or trailing spaces in the data.

- The `BETWEEN` operator simplifies range selection and can improve query readability when dealing with ranges.

- If you have a large dataset and frequently use `BETWEEN`, consider indexing the columns you use for range filtering to improve query performance.

- The `BETWEEN` operator is inclusive, so it will include the values at both ends of the specified range.

- Use `BETWEEN` with care when working with floating-point numbers, as precision issues might lead to unexpected results.

6.10 EXISTS

Description:

The SQL `EXISTS` operator is used to check the existence of rows in a subquery. It returns `TRUE` if the subquery returns one or more rows; otherwise, it returns `FALSE`. The `EXISTS` operator is often used in conjunction with a correlated subquery to perform conditional actions based on the existence of certain data.

Syntax:

```sql
SELECT column1, column2, ...

FROM table_name

WHERE EXISTS (subquery);
```

- `column1`, `column2`, ...: The columns you want to retrieve.

- `table_name`: The table you are querying.

- `subquery`: The subquery that checks for the existence of certain rows.

Example:

Let's say you want to find all customers who have placed orders in the `Orders` table.

```sql
SELECT CustomerName

FROM Customers

WHERE EXISTS (

  SELECT 1

  FROM Orders

  WHERE Customers.CustomerID = Orders.CustomerID

);
```

Explanation of the Code:

- The SQL query selects the `CustomerName` column from the `Customers` table.

- The `WHERE` clause contains a subquery. This subquery checks for the existence of at least one row in the `Orders` table where the `CustomerID` matches between the `Customers` and `Orders` tables.

- If the subquery returns one or more rows (i.e., if there are customers who have placed orders), the main query will include those customers in the result set.

Tips:

- The `EXISTS` operator is used to determine the existence of rows based on a subquery.

- The subquery typically returns a value of `1` for each row that meets the condition. The main query then checks whether any `1` exists in the result.

- When used with correlated subqueries, the `EXISTS` operator can help filter or conditionally include rows based on related data.

- You can also use `NOT EXISTS` to check for the non-existence of rows in a subquery.

- Be careful when using `EXISTS` with correlated subqueries, as it can impact query performance. Ensure your database is properly indexed for optimal performance.

- The `EXISTS` operator is often used in combination with other SQL clauses, such as `SELECT`, `FROM`, and `WHERE`, to perform conditional actions.

6.11 ANY / SOME

Description:

The SQL `ANY` and `SOME` operators are used to compare a value to a set of values in a subquery. They return `TRUE` if the comparison is true for at least one row in the subquery's result set, and `FALSE` otherwise. These operators are typically used in conjunction with a comparison operator like `=`, `>`, `<`, `>=`, or `<=` to compare a value with multiple values in a subquery.

Syntax:

```sql
expression operator ANY (subquery)
```

- `expression`: The value you want to compare.

- `operator`: A comparison operator like `=`, `>`, `<`, `>=`, or `<=`.

- `subquery`: The subquery that provides a set of values for comparison.

Example:

Suppose you want to find all employees whose salary is greater than the lowest salary in the `Salaries` table.

```sql
```

```
SELECT EmployeeName, Salary

FROM Employees

WHERE Salary > ANY (

  SELECT MIN(Salary)

  FROM Salaries

);
```

Explanation of the Code:

- The SQL query selects the `EmployeeName` and `Salary` columns from the `Employees` table.

- The `WHERE` clause contains a condition where the `Salary` of each employee is compared to `ANY` of the values returned by the subquery.

- The subquery calculates the minimum salary (`MIN(Salary)`) from the `Salaries` table. It will return a single value, the lowest salary.

- The comparison operator (`>`) checks if the employee's salary is greater than at least one of the values from the subquery, which, in this case, is the lowest salary.

Tips:

- Use the `ANY` or `SOME` operator when you want to compare a value with multiple values in a subquery.

- These operators can be combined with various comparison operators, including `=`, `>`, `<`, `>=`, and `<=`.

- The subquery should return a set of values (a result set) for comparison. You can use aggregate functions like `MIN`, `MAX`, `SUM`, etc., in the subquery.

- The comparison is evaluated as `TRUE` if the condition is met for at least one row in the subquery's result set.

- Be cautious when using these operators, as they can affect query performance. Ensure your database is properly indexed for optimal performance.

- You can also use `ALL` to check if the condition is true for all rows in the subquery's result set.

6.12 ALL

Description:

The SQL `ALL` operator is used to compare a value to all values in a subquery. It returns `TRUE` if the comparison is true for all rows in the subquery's result set and `FALSE` if the comparison is not true for any row. The `ALL` operator is typically used in conjunction with a comparison operator like `=`, `>`, `<`, `>=`, or `<=` to compare a value with all values in a subquery.

Syntax:

```sql
expression operator ALL (subquery)
```

- `expression`: The value you want to compare.

- `operator`: A comparison operator like `=`, `>`, `<`, `>=`, or `<=`.

- `subquery`: The subquery that provides a set of values for comparison.

Example:

Suppose you want to find all employees whose salary is greater than or equal to all the salaries in the `Salaries` table.

```sql
SELECT EmployeeName, Salary
```

```
FROM Employees

WHERE Salary >= ALL (

  SELECT Salary

  FROM Salaries

);
```
```

**Explanation of the Code:**

- The SQL query selects the `EmployeeName` and `Salary` columns from the `Employees` table.

- The `WHERE` clause contains a condition where the `Salary` of each employee is compared to `ALL` of the values returned by the subquery.

- The subquery selects all `Salary` values from the `Salaries` table.

- The comparison operator (`>=`) checks if the employee's salary is greater than or equal to all the values from the subquery, which, in this case, are all the salaries from the `Salaries` table.

**Tips:**

- Use the `ALL` operator when you want to compare a value with all values in a subquery.

- These operators can be combined with various comparison operators, including `=`, `>`, `<`, `>=`, and `<=`.

- The subquery should return a set of values (a result set) for comparison.

- The comparison is evaluated as `TRUE` only if the condition is met for all rows in the subquery's result set.
```

- Be cautious when using these operators, as they can affect query performance. Ensure your database is properly indexed for optimal performance.

VII.
Formatting functions

7.1 CONCAT()

Description:

The SQL `CONCAT()` function is used to concatenate two or more strings into a single string. It allows you to combine text from multiple columns, variables, or literal values into a single string.

Syntax:

```sql
CONCAT(string1, string2, ...)
```

- `string1`, `string2`, ...: These are the strings you want to concatenate. You can provide two or more strings to concatenate.

Example:

Let's say you have a table named `Students` with the following columns: `FirstName`, `LastName`, and `StudentID`. You want to create a single column that contains the full name of each student by concatenating the first name and last name.

```sql
SELECT CONCAT(FirstName, ' ', LastName) AS FullName

FROM Students;
```

Explanation of the Code:

- The SQL query selects the `FirstName` and `LastName` columns from the `Students` table.

- The `CONCAT()` function is used to concatenate the `FirstName` and `LastName` columns, separated by a space character (' ').

- The result is given an alias `FullName`, so the output column is named `FullName`.

Tips:

- Use the `CONCAT()` function to join strings or column values together.

- You can provide as many strings or values as you want to concatenate.

- You can include literal values (e.g., spaces or punctuation) between the columns or strings to separate them in the output.

- If any of the values are `NULL`, the `CONCAT()` function returns `NULL`. You can use the `COALESCE()` function to handle `NULL` values if needed.

7.2 CONCAT_WS()

Description:

The SQL `CONCAT_WS()` function is used to concatenate multiple strings with a specified separator. It allows you to join strings together while including a separator between them.

Syntax:

```sql
CONCAT_WS(separator, string1, string2, ...)
```

- `separator`: This is the string that you want to use as a separator between the concatenated strings.

- `string1`, `string2`, ...: These are the strings you want to concatenate and separate with the `separator`.

Example:

Suppose you have a table named `Employees` with the following columns: `FirstName`, `LastName`, and `JobTitle`. You want to create a single column that contains the full name of each employee, followed by their job title, separated by a comma and space.

```sql
SELECT CONCAT_WS(', ', CONCAT(FirstName, ' ', LastName), JobTitle) AS EmployeeInfo
FROM Employees;
```

```

```

Explanation of the Code:

- The SQL query selects the `FirstName`, `LastName`, and `JobTitle` columns from the `Employees` table.

- The `CONCAT_WS()` function is used to concatenate the `FirstName` and `LastName` columns with a space (' ') as the separator. Then, it concatenates the result with the `JobTitle` column using a comma and a space (', ') as the separator.

- The result is given an alias `EmployeeInfo`, so the output column is named `EmployeeInfo`.

Tips:

- Use the `CONCAT_WS()` function when you need to concatenate strings while specifying a separator.

- You can include multiple strings and separators in the function call.

- The separator is only added between non-NULL values, and NULL values are ignored in the concatenation.

- This function is helpful when you want to format strings for display or for exporting data, such as generating CSV files.

- Make sure to include the separators as string literals (e.g., ', ') in the function call.

7.3 FORMAT()

Description:

The SQL `FORMAT()` function is used to format numbers, dates, and times into a specific format. This function is often used to make data more human-readable and present it in a well-defined format.

Syntax:

```sql
FORMAT(value, format)
```

- `value`: The value you want to format. It can be a number, date, time, or datetime.

- `format`: The format string specifying how you want to format the `value`.

Example:

Suppose you have a table named `Sales` with a column named `OrderDate` containing date values. You want to format these date values to display in the "Month dd, yyyy" format.

```sql
SELECT FORMAT(OrderDate, 'MMMM dd, yyyy') AS FormattedDate
FROM Sales;
```

Explanation of the Code:

- The SQL query selects the `OrderDate` column from the `Sales` table.

- The `FORMAT()` function is used to format the `OrderDate` values using the 'MMMM dd, yyyy' format string. In this format string:

  - `"MMMM"` represents the full month name.

  - `"dd"` represents the day of the month with leading zeros.

  - `"yyyy"` represents the four-digit year.

- The result is given an alias `FormattedDate`, which is the name of the output column.

Tips:

- The `FORMAT()` function is available in SQL Server and some other database management systems. It might not be available in all database systems, so check your database system's documentation to see if it is supported.

- The `format` string allows you to define how the value should be displayed. You can use various placeholders for different parts of the value (e.g., 'yyyy' for the year, 'MM' for the month, 'dd' for the day).

- The format string can vary depending on the database system and its supported date and time format codes. Make sure to use the format codes that are compatible with your database system.

- Be cautious when formatting dates, as different database systems may have different rules for handling date formats and regional settings.

- The `FORMAT()` function is useful when you want to customize the display of dates, numbers, or times for reports or user interfaces. It provides a way to present data in a user-friendly manner.

7.4 DATE_FORMAT()

Description:

The SQL `DATE_FORMAT()` function is used to format date and time values into a specific format. It allows you to convert a date or time value into a human-readable string using a defined format pattern. This function is typically used for displaying dates and times in a user-friendly manner in the desired format.

Syntax:

The basic syntax of the `DATE_FORMAT()` function is as follows:

```sql
DATE_FORMAT(date, format)
```

- `date`: The date or datetime value that you want to format.

- `format`: The format string specifying how you want to format the `date` value.

Example:

Suppose you have a table named `Orders` with a column named `OrderDate` containing datetime values. You want to format these datetime values to display only the date in the "YYYY-MM-DD" format.

```sql
SELECT DATE_FORMAT(OrderDate, '%Y-%m-%d') AS FormattedDate
FROM Orders;
```

Explanation of the Code:

- The SQL query selects the `OrderDate` column from the `Orders` table.

- The `DATE_FORMAT()` function is used to format the `OrderDate` values using the '%Y-%m-%d' format string. In this format string:

  - `%Y` represents the four-digit year.

  - `%m` represents the month with leading zeros.

  - `%d` represents the day of the month with leading zeros.

- The result is given an alias `FormattedDate`, which is the name of the output column.

Tips:

- The `DATE_FORMAT()` function is commonly used in MySQL, but it may not be available in all database management systems. Make sure to check your specific database system's documentation for date and time formatting functions.

- The `format` string can include various format codes that represent different parts of the date and time values. For example, `%Y` for year, `%m` for month, `%d` for day, `%H` for hours, `%i` for minutes, and so on.

- The format string is case-sensitive, so `%Y` is different from `%y`. `%Y` represents the full year (e.g., 2023), while `%y` represents the last two digits of the year (e.g., 23).

- The `DATE_FORMAT()` function is useful for customizing the display of dates and times in reports or user interfaces. It allows you to present date and time data in a format that is easy to read and understand.

- Depending on your database system, you may need to use different format codes or patterns. Be aware of the database-specific syntax for date and time formatting.

7.5 TO_CHAR()

Description:

The SQL `TO_CHAR()` function is used to format a date, time, or timestamp as a string in a specific format. It is primarily used for formatting date and time values for display in a human-readable format. This function is commonly found in databases like Oracle and PostgreSQL.

Syntax:

The basic syntax of the `TO_CHAR()` function is as follows:

```sql
TO_CHAR(date, format)
```

- `date`: The date, time, or timestamp value that you want to format.
- `format`: The format pattern that defines how the `date` value should be formatted.

Example:

Suppose you have a table named `Events` with a column named `EventDate` containing timestamp values. You want to format these timestamp values to display only the date in the "YYYY-MM-DD" format.

```sql
```

```sql
SELECT TO_CHAR(EventDate, 'YYYY-MM-DD') AS FormattedDate
FROM Events;
```

Explanation of the Code:

- The SQL query selects the `EventDate` column from the `Events` table.

- The `TO_CHAR()` function is used to format the `EventDate` values using the 'YYYY-MM-DD' format. In this format string:

  - `YYYY` represents the four-digit year.

  - `MM` represents the two-digit month with leading zeros.

  - `DD` represents the two-digit day of the month with leading zeros.

- The result is given an alias `FormattedDate`, which is the name of the output column.

Tips:

- The `TO_CHAR()` function is commonly used in databases like Oracle and PostgreSQL. However, its availability may vary depending on the database system you are using. Be sure to consult your specific database system's documentation for date and time formatting functions.

- The `format` parameter allows you to specify a wide range of format codes, such as `YYYY` for the year, `MM` for the month, `DD` for the day, `HH` for hours, `MI` for minutes, and more.

- The format codes are case-sensitive. For example, `YYYY` is different from `yyyy`, and `MM` is different from `mm`. Make sure to use the correct case for the desired format.

- The `TO_CHAR()` function is a powerful tool for customizing how date and time values are displayed in your SQL query results. It enables you to present date and time data in a user-friendly format.

- Be aware that the available format codes and patterns may vary between database systems. Always check the documentation for your specific database system when working with date and time formatting.

7.6 CAST()

Description:

The SQL `CAST()` function is used to explicitly convert an expression of one data type to another data type. This function is particularly useful when you want to ensure that data is represented in a specific format or type, or when you need to perform operations on data in a consistent manner.

Syntax:

The basic syntax of the `CAST()` function is as follows:

```sql
CAST(expression AS data_type)
```

- `expression`: The value or expression you want to convert.
- `data_type`: The target data type to which you want to cast or convert the expression.

Example:

Let's say you have a table named `Products`, and it contains a column named `Price` with data stored as text (varchar). You want to perform a numeric comparison on the `Price` values by casting them to a numeric data type.

```sql
SELECT ProductName, CAST(Price AS DECIMAL(10, 2)) AS NumericPrice
FROM Products
WHERE CAST(Price AS DECIMAL(10, 2)) > 50.00;
```

Explanation of the Code:

- The SQL query selects the `ProductName` column from the `Products` table.

- The `CAST()` function is used to convert the `Price` column from its original varchar data type to a decimal data type with 10 total digits and 2 decimal places. This ensures that the `Price` values are treated as numbers for comparison.

- The `WHERE` clause filters the rows where the `NumericPrice` is greater than 50.00, which is now possible because of the cast to a numeric data type.

Tips:

- Use the `CAST()` function when you need to perform operations or comparisons on values that are stored in a different data type than what you require for the operation. It ensures that the data is presented in a consistent and compatible format.

- Be cautious when casting between data types. Make sure that the conversion makes sense for your data. Casting from one data type to another may result in data loss or unexpected behavior if not done correctly.

- The `data_type` you specify in the `CAST()` function should be a valid data type in your database system, and it should be compatible with the source data type you are trying to cast.

- Different database systems may have slightly different ways of handling type casting, so consult your specific database system's documentation for any unique features or nuances.

- The `CAST()` function is commonly used for converting between data types like varchar to numeric, varchar to date, and so on. It is a powerful tool to ensure data consistency in your SQL queries.

7.7 CONVERT()

Description:

The SQL `CONVERT()` function is used to convert an expression or value from one data type to another. It is similar to the `CAST()` function and serves the purpose of explicitly specifying the target data type for the conversion. `CONVERT()` is commonly used to ensure that data is presented in a specific format or type, which can be important for various database operations.

Syntax:

The basic syntax of the `CONVERT()` function is as follows:

```sql
CONVERT(data_type, expression, style)
```

- `data_type`: The target data type to which you want to convert the expression.

- `expression`: The value or expression you want to convert.

- `style` (optional): Some database systems, like Microsoft SQL Server, allow an additional style parameter that specifies the format of the converted data. This parameter is optional and may not be supported in all database systems.

Example:

Suppose you have a table named `Orders`, and it contains a column named `OrderDate` with data stored as text (varchar). You want to convert the `OrderDate` values to the `DATE` data type for better date manipulation.

```sql
SELECT OrderID, CONVERT(DATE, OrderDate) AS ConvertedDate
FROM Orders;
```

Explanation of the Code:

- The SQL query selects the `OrderID` column from the `Orders` table.

- The `CONVERT()` function is used to convert the `OrderDate` column from its original varchar data type to the DATE data type. This ensures that the `OrderDate` values are treated as dates.

Tips:

- The `CONVERT()` function is similar to the `CAST()` function but may be more flexible in certain database systems, especially when an additional style parameter is available. The choice between `CAST()` and `CONVERT()` may depend on your specific database system's requirements.

- Ensure that the `data_type` you specify in the `CONVERT()` function is a valid data type in your database system and is compatible with the source data type you are trying to convert.

- Be cautious when converting between data types, as the conversion may result in data loss or unexpected behavior if not done correctly.

- If your database system supports the `style` parameter, it can be used to control the format of the converted data. This is particularly useful for date and time conversions where different styles may represent dates differently (e.g., 'MM/DD/YYYY' vs. 'DD/MM/YYYY').

- The `CONVERT()` function is commonly used for converting between data types such as varchar to numeric, varchar to date, and so on. It can be a valuable tool to ensure data consistency in your SQL queries.

7.8 LTRIM()

Description:

The SQL `LTRIM()` function is used to remove any leading (on the left side) spaces or specified characters from a string. It's often used when you want to clean up data stored in a database by removing any unnecessary whitespace from the beginning of a text value.

Syntax:

The basic syntax of the `LTRIM()` function is as follows:

```sql
LTRIM(string)
```

- `string`: The string or column from which you want to remove leading spaces or characters.

Example:

Suppose you have a table named `Employee` with a column `FirstName` that contains some values with leading spaces. You want to retrieve the first names with the leading spaces removed.

```sql
SELECT LTRIM(FirstName) AS CleanFirstName
FROM Employee;
```

```

**Explanation of the Code:**

- The SQL query selects the `FirstName` column from the `Employee` table.

- The `LTRIM()` function is applied to the `FirstName` column. It removes any leading spaces from each value in the column.

- The result is returned as `CleanFirstName`, which contains the first names with leading spaces removed.

**Tips:**

- The `LTRIM()` function is a helpful tool for cleaning up text data, particularly when dealing with user input or data imports where extra spaces can be common.

- It is important to note that `LTRIM()` only removes leading spaces or characters. If you also need to remove trailing spaces or characters from the end of a string, you can use the `RTRIM()` function. If you need to remove spaces or characters from both the beginning and the end of a string, you can use the `TRIM()` function, if supported by your database system.

- Make sure to use `LTRIM()` on the appropriate columns or strings where you need to eliminate leading spaces. It's commonly used in SELECT statements to present cleaner data for reporting or display.
```

- When you're dealing with character data, you may also want to consider the `DATALENGTH()` or `LEN()` function to check the length of strings before and after using `LTRIM()` to ensure spaces have been removed as expected.

7.9 RTRIM()

Description:

The SQL `RTRIM()` function is used to remove any trailing (on the right side) spaces or specified characters from a string. It's often used when you want to clean up data stored in a database by removing any unnecessary whitespace from the end of a text value.

Syntax:

The basic syntax of the `RTRIM()` function is as follows:

```sql
RTRIM(string)
```

- `string`: The string or column from which you want to remove trailing spaces or characters.

Example:

Suppose you have a table named `Product` with a column `ProductName` that contains some values with trailing spaces. You want to retrieve the product names with the trailing spaces removed.

```sql
SELECT RTRIM(ProductName) AS CleanProductName
```

FROM Product;
```

**Explanation of the Code:**

- The SQL query selects the `ProductName` column from the `Product` table.

- The `RTRIM()` function is applied to the `ProductName` column. It removes any trailing spaces from each value in the column.

- The result is returned as `CleanProductName`, which contains the product names with trailing spaces removed.

**Tips:**

- The `RTRIM()` function is a helpful tool for cleaning up text data, particularly when dealing with user input or data imports where extra spaces can be common.

- It is important to note that `RTRIM()` only removes trailing spaces or characters. If you also need to remove leading spaces or characters from the beginning of a string, you can use the `LTRIM()` function. If you need to remove spaces or characters from both the beginning and the end of a string, you can use the `TRIM()` function, if supported by your database system.

- Make sure to use `RTRIM()` on the appropriate columns or strings where you need to eliminate trailing spaces. It's commonly used in SELECT statements to present cleaner data for reporting or display.
```

- When you're dealing with character data, you may also want to consider the `DATALENGTH()` or `LEN()` function to check the length of strings before and after using `RTRIM()` to ensure spaces have been removed as expected.

7.10 TRIM()

Description:

The SQL `TRIM()` function is used to remove leading (on the left side), trailing (on the right side), or both leading and trailing spaces or specified characters from a string. This function is commonly used to clean up text data by removing any unnecessary whitespace or characters from the beginning and end of a string.

Syntax:

The basic syntax of the `TRIM()` function is as follows:

```sql
TRIM([BOTH | LEADING | TRAILING] [trim_character FROM] string)
```

- `BOTH`, `LEADING`, or `TRAILING`: Optional. Specifies which part of the string to trim. `BOTH` trims from both sides, `LEADING` trims from the left side, and `TRAILING` trims from the right side. If not specified, it trims from both sides by default.

- `trim_character`: Optional. Specifies the characters to be removed from the string. If not specified, it removes spaces by default.

- `string`: The string or column from which you want to remove leading, trailing, or both spaces or characters.

Example:

Suppose you have a table named `Employee` with a column `Name` that contains some values with leading and trailing spaces. You want to retrieve the employee names with the leading and trailing spaces removed.

```sql
SELECT TRIM(BOTH ' ' FROM Name) AS CleanName
FROM Employee;
```

Explanation of the Code:

- The SQL query selects the `Name` column from the `Employee` table.

- The `TRIM()` function is applied to the `Name` column with `BOTH ' '`, specifying to remove spaces from both the beginning and end of each value in the column.

- The result is returned as `CleanName`, which contains the employee names with leading and trailing spaces removed.

Tips:

- The `TRIM()` function is a powerful tool for cleaning up text data, especially when you need to eliminate leading and trailing spaces. You can also specify specific characters to be removed by providing a `trim_character`.

- Be cautious about removing characters using `TRIM()` as it can result in data loss. It's essential to understand your data and the effect of trimming specific characters.

- Depending on your database system, you may need to use different syntax or functions to achieve the same result. Check your database's documentation for variations of `TRIM()`.

- The `RTRIM()` and `LTRIM()` functions can be used separately to remove only trailing or leading spaces, respectively. If you want to remove only trailing spaces, use `RTRIM()`. If you want to remove only leading spaces, use `LTRIM()`.

- Always make sure you have a backup of your data or that you're working with a copy when performing operations that modify your data. This helps prevent accidental data loss.

7.11 UPPER()

Description:

The SQL `UPPER()` function is used to convert all the characters in a given string or column to uppercase. This function is particularly useful when you want to standardize the case of text data, making it easier to compare, search, or format text consistently.

Syntax:

The syntax for the `UPPER()` function is straightforward:

```sql
UPPER(string)
```

- `string`: This is the text or string expression that you want to convert to uppercase.

Example Usage:

Let's say you have a table named `Employees` with a column called `employee_name`, and you want to retrieve all employee names in uppercase:

```sql
SELECT UPPER(employee_name) AS uppercase_name
FROM Employees;
```

```

**Explanation of the Code:**

- The SQL query selects the `employee_name` column and converts it to uppercase using the `UPPER()` function.

- It aliases the resulting uppercase text as `uppercase_name` in the output.

- The query returns a result set with employee names in uppercase.

**Tips:**

- The `UPPER()` function is case-insensitive and will convert all characters to uppercase, regardless of their original case.

- You can use the `UPPER()` function in various SQL statements, such as `SELECT`, `UPDATE`, or `INSERT`, whenever you need to work with uppercase text.

- Be cautious when using the `UPPER()` function in search or comparison operations. Since it converts all characters to uppercase, it may affect case-sensitive searches.

- If you need to perform case-insensitive searches, you can use the `UPPER()` function to convert both the column value and the search term to uppercase. For example:

```sql
SELECT * FROM Products WHERE UPPER(product_name) = UPPER('widget');
```
```

```

This query would retrieve products with the name 'widget,' regardless of the case of the search term.


- The `UPPER()` function can also be combined with other functions or expressions to manipulate text data in SQL. For example, you can concatenate strings, trim whitespace, or perform other text transformations along with uppercase conversion.
```

7.12 LOWER()

Description:

The SQL `LOWER()` function is used to convert all characters in a string to lowercase. This function is useful when you want to standardize the case of text data, making it easier to compare and manipulate text in a case-insensitive manner.

Syntax:

The basic syntax of the `LOWER()` function is as follows:

```sql
LOWER(string)
```

- `string`: The string or column that you want to convert to lowercase.

Example:

Suppose you have a table named `Products` with a column `ProductName` that contains product names with varying letter cases. You want to retrieve the product names in all lowercase.

```sql
SELECT LOWER(ProductName) AS LowercaseProductName
FROM Products;
```

```
```

Explanation of the Code:

- The SQL query selects the `ProductName` column from the `Products` table.

- The `LOWER()` function is applied to the `ProductName` column, which converts all characters in each product name to lowercase.

- The result is returned as `LowercaseProductName`, containing the product names in all lowercase.

Tips:

- The `LOWER()` function is a straightforward way to convert text to lowercase, which can be particularly useful for case-insensitive text comparisons and uniform text formatting.

- Be aware that some database systems may have different functions for converting text to lowercase, such as `LCASE()` or `LCase()` in some systems.

- To convert text to uppercase, you can use the `UPPER()` function.

- The `LOWER()` function only converts alphabetical characters to lowercase. Non-alphabetical characters and digits remain unchanged.

- When using the `LOWER()` function in queries, remember that it's not altering the original data in the table. It's only altering the display of the data in the query result.

- If you need to permanently change the case of data in a table, you would need to use an `UPDATE` statement to modify the data.

- Carefully consider the collation (character set and sorting rules) of your database when working with case-insensitive text data. Collation settings can impact the behavior of case conversions and comparisons.

7.13 INITCAP()

Description:

The SQL `INITCAP()` function is used to convert the first character of each word in a string to uppercase and the remaining characters to lowercase. This function is typically used to standardize the capitalization of text data, making it more visually appealing and easier to read.

Syntax:

The basic syntax of the `INITCAP()` function is as follows:

```sql
INITCAP(string)
```

- `string`: The string or column that you want to convert to an "init-capped" format, where the first letter of each word is in uppercase.

Example:

Suppose you have a table named `Employees` with columns `FirstName` and `LastName`, and you want to retrieve the full names of employees with the first letter of each name in uppercase.

```sql
SELECT INITCAP(FirstName) || ' ' || INITCAP(LastName) AS FullName
```

```
FROM Employees;
```
```

**Explanation of the Code:**

- The SQL query selects the `FirstName` and `LastName` columns from the `Employees` table.

- The `INITCAP()` function is applied to both `FirstName` and `LastName` columns, which converts the first letter of each word (name) to uppercase and the rest to lowercase.

- The `||` operator is used for string concatenation to form the full name with a space in between.

- The result is returned as `FullName`, containing the full names of employees with the first letter of each name in uppercase.

**Tips:**

- The `INITCAP()` function is useful for making text data more visually consistent and appealing, especially when presenting names or titles.

- The `INITCAP()` function typically capitalizes the first letter of each word in the input string. Words are considered to be separated by spaces.

- The `INITCAP()` function does not affect special characters or digits, and it only capitalizes alphabetical characters.
```

- Be cautious with this function when dealing with data from different languages and character sets, as the definition of a "word" may vary across languages and collations.

- This function is available in some database systems like PostgreSQL and Oracle, but it may not be available in others. Be sure to check the documentation of your specific database management system for compatibility.

7.14 LPAD()

Description:

The SQL `LPAD()` function, which stands for "left pad," is used to add a specified character or a sequence of characters to the beginning (left side) of a string until it reaches a specified length. This function is commonly used for formatting and aligning strings to a specific length, especially when dealing with fixed-width data or reports.

Syntax:

The basic syntax of the `LPAD()` function is as follows:

```sql
LPAD(string, length, padding)
```

- `string`: The input string that you want to pad.

- `length`: The total desired length of the result after padding.

- `padding`: The character or sequence of characters to add to the left side of the input string until it reaches the desired length.

Example:

Suppose you have a table named `Orders` with a column named `OrderID`, and you want to display the order IDs as five-character strings, left-padded with zeros.

```sql
SELECT LPAD(OrderID, 5, '0') AS PaddedOrderID

FROM Orders;
```

Explanation of the Code:

- The SQL query selects the `OrderID` column from the `Orders` table.

- The `LPAD()` function is applied to the `OrderID` column with the following arguments:

  - `OrderID` is the input string to pad.

  - `5` is the desired total length of the result after padding (in this case, a five-character string).

  - `'0'` is the character to add to the left side of the input string until it reaches the desired length. In this example, it's the character '0'.

- The result is returned as `PaddedOrderID`, which displays the order IDs as five-character strings, left-padded with zeros.

Tips:

- The `LPAD()` function is helpful for formatting and aligning strings in reports or when working with data that requires fixed-width columns.

- The `length` argument specifies the total length of the result string after padding. If the original string is longer than the desired length, no padding is applied, and the original string remains unchanged.

- The `padding` argument can be a single character (e.g., '0') or a longer sequence of characters. It's used to pad the input string until it reaches the specified length.

- You can use the `RPAD()` function for right padding, which adds characters to the right side of a string to reach a desired length.

- Depending on your database system, the `LPAD()` function may have slight variations in syntax and behavior. Be sure to consult your database's documentation for specific details.

7.15 RPAD()

Description:

The SQL `RPAD()` function, which stands for "right pad," is used to add a specified character or a sequence of characters to the end (right side) of a string until it reaches a specified length. This function is commonly used for formatting and aligning strings to a specific length, especially when dealing with fixed-width data or reports.

Syntax:

The basic syntax of the `RPAD()` function is as follows:

```sql
RPAD(string, length, padding)
```

- `string`: The input string that you want to pad.

- `length`: The total desired length of the result after padding.

- `padding`: The character or sequence of characters to add to the right side of the input string until it reaches the desired length.

Example:

Suppose you have a table named `Products` with a column named `ProductName`, and you want to display the product names as 20-character strings, right-padded with spaces.

```sql
SELECT RPAD(ProductName, 20, ' ') AS PaddedProductName
FROM Products;
```

Explanation of the Code:

- The SQL query selects the `ProductName` column from the `Products` table.

- The `RPAD()` function is applied to the `ProductName` column with the following arguments:

  - `ProductName` is the input string to pad.

  - `20` is the desired total length of the result after padding (in this case, a 20-character string).

  - `' '` (a single space) is the character to add to the right side of the input string until it reaches the desired length.

- The result is returned as `PaddedProductName`, which displays the product names as 20-character strings, right-padded with spaces.

Tips:

- The `RPAD()` function is helpful for formatting and aligning strings in reports or when working with data that requires fixed-width columns.

- The `length` argument specifies the total length of the result string after padding. If the original string is longer than the desired length, no padding is applied, and the original string remains unchanged.

- The `padding` argument can be a single character (e.g., ' ') or a longer sequence of characters. It's used to pad the input string until it reaches the specified length.

- You can use the `LPAD()` function for left padding, which adds characters to the left side of a string to reach a desired length.

- Depending on your database system, the `RPAD()` function may have slight variations in syntax and behavior. Be sure to consult your database's documentation for specific details.

7.16 REPLACE()

Description:

The SQL `REPLACE()` function is used to replace all occurrences of a specified substring within a string with another substring. This function is helpful for modifying string data, such as changing specific characters or patterns in text.

Syntax:

The basic syntax of the `REPLACE()` function is as follows:

```sql
REPLACE(string, old_substring, new_substring)
```

- `string`: The input string where you want to replace occurrences of a substring.

- `old_substring`: The substring you want to find and replace.

- `new_substring`: The substring you want to replace `old_substring` with.

Example:

Let's say you have a table named `Customers` with a column named `Address`, and you want to replace occurrences of "St." with "Street" in the addresses.

```sql
```

```
SELECT REPLACE(Address, 'St.', 'Street') AS UpdatedAddress
FROM Customers;
```

Explanation of the Code:

- The SQL query selects the `Address` column from the `Customers` table.

- The `REPLACE()` function is applied to the `Address` column with the following arguments:

  - `Address` is the input string where you want to replace occurrences of a substring.

  - `'St.'` is the old substring you want to find and replace.

  - `'Street'` is the new substring you want to replace 'St.' with.

- The result is returned as `UpdatedAddress`, which displays the addresses with "St." replaced by "Street."

Tips:

- The `REPLACE()` function is useful for modifying text data, such as correcting typos, standardizing formatting, or changing specific patterns in strings.

- The `old_substring` and `new_substring` arguments are case-sensitive. If you want to perform a case-insensitive replacement, you may need to use functions specific to your database system (e.g., `REPLACE` for MySQL and `REPLACE` with the `COLLATE` clause for SQL Server).

- You can use the `REPLACE()` function within SQL queries, but it's also commonly used in programming languages to manipulate strings before constructing SQL queries.

- If the `old_substring` occurs multiple times within the `string`, all occurrences are replaced with the `new_substring`.

- Keep in mind that the `REPLACE()` function works on the entire string, so you should be cautious to avoid unintentional replacements that may affect parts of the string you don't intend to modify.

7.17 SUBSTRING() / SUBSTR()

Description:

The SQL `SUBSTRING()` function, also known as `SUBSTR()`, is used to extract a portion of a string based on a specified starting position and, optionally, a specified length. It is often used to manipulate string data by ex **n:**tracting substrings from a larger string.

Syntax:

The basic syntax of the `SUBSTRING()` or `SUBSTR()` function is as follows:

```sql
SUBSTRING(string, start_position, length)
```

- `string`: The input string from which you want to extract a substring.

- `start_position`: The starting position within the `string` from where you want to begin the extraction. The position is 1-based.

- `length` (optional): The number of characters to extract from the `string`. If omitted, the function extracts from the `start_position` to the end of the `string`.

Example:

Suppose you have a table named `Products` with a column named `ProductName`, and you want to extract the first 5 characters from the product names.

```sql
SELECT SUBSTRING(ProductName, 1, 5) AS ShortProductName

FROM Products;
```

Explanation of the Code:

- The SQL query selects the `ProductName` column from the `Products` table.

- The `SUBSTRING()` function is applied to the `ProductName` column with the following arguments:

  - `ProductName` is the input string from which you want to extract a substring.

  - `1` is the starting position (the first character) from where you want to begin the extraction.

  - `5` is the length, which specifies that you want to extract the first 5 characters.

- The result is returned as `ShortProductName`, which displays the first 5 characters of the product names.

Tips:

- The `SUBSTRING()` or `SUBSTR()` function is versatile and can be used for various purposes, such as extracting parts of text, parsing data, or formatting string values.

- The `start_position` argument specifies where to begin the extraction, and it's 1-based, meaning that a value of 1 corresponds to the first character in the string.

- If you omit the `length` argument, the function extracts from the `start_position` to the end of the string.

- You can use negative values for the `start_position` to count from the end of the string. For example, `-1` represents the last character, `-2` is the second-to-last character, and so on.

- Be cautious when using the `SUBSTRING()` function, especially when specifying the `start_position` and `length`, to avoid errors or unexpected results. Ensure that the values are within the boundaries of the string.

- Different database systems may have slight variations in the usage of the `SUBSTRING()` or `SUBSTR()` function, so refer to your specific database's documentation for any differences in implementation.

7.18 LEFT()

Description:

The SQL `LEFT()` function is used to extract a specified number of characters from the beginning (left) of a string. This function is particularly useful when you need to work with the leftmost characters of a text field or column.

Syntax:

The basic syntax of the `LEFT()` function is as follows:

```sql
LEFT(string, length)
```

- `string`: The input string from which you want to extract characters from the left.
- `length`: The number of characters to extract from the beginning (left) of the `string`.

Example:

Suppose you have a table named `Employees` with a column named `FullName`, and you want to extract the first 10 characters (leftmost characters) from each full name.

```sql
SELECT LEFT(FullName, 10) AS ShortName
```

FROM Employees;
```

**Explanation of the Code:**

- The SQL query selects the `FullName` column from the `Employees` table.

- The `LEFT()` function is applied to the `FullName` column with the following arguments:

  - `FullName` is the input string from which you want to extract characters from the left.

  - `10` is the `length`, which specifies that you want to extract the first 10 characters.

- The result is returned as `ShortName`, which displays the first 10 characters from each full name.

**Tips:**

- The `LEFT()` function is a simple way to extract a fixed number of characters from the beginning of a string.

- Be cautious when specifying the `length` argument to ensure that it accurately reflects the number of characters you want to extract. If you provide a value larger than the length of the string, it will return the entire string.

- Consider using the `LEFT()` function for various purposes such as truncating long text, creating abbreviated labels, or extracting prefixes from data.
```

- Depending on your database system, the `LEFT()` function might have variations in its usage, so it's a good practice to refer to your specific database's documentation for any differences in implementation.

7.19 RIGHT()

Description:

The SQL `RIGHT()` function is used to extract a specified number of characters from the end (right) of a string. This function is especially useful when you need to work with the rightmost characters of a text field or column.

Syntax:

The basic syntax of the `RIGHT()` function is as follows:

```sql
RIGHT(string, length)
```

- `string`: The input string from which you want to extract characters from the right.
- `length`: The number of characters to extract from the end (right) of the `string`.

Example:

Suppose you have a table named `Products` with a column named `ProductCode`, and you want to extract the last 5 characters (rightmost characters) from each product code.

```sql
SELECT RIGHT(ProductCode, 5) AS ShortCode
```

FROM Products;
```

**Explanation of the Code:**

- The SQL query selects the `ProductCode` column from the `Products` table.

- The `RIGHT()` function is applied to the `ProductCode` column with the following arguments:

  - `ProductCode` is the input string from which you want to extract characters from the right.

  - `5` is the `length`, which specifies that you want to extract the last 5 characters.

- The result is returned as `ShortCode`, which displays the last 5 characters from each product code.

**Tips:**

- The `RIGHT()` function is a simple way to extract a fixed number of characters from the end of a string.

- Be careful when specifying the `length` argument to ensure that it accurately reflects the number of characters you want to extract. If you provide a value larger than the length of the string, it will return the entire string.

- Consider using the `RIGHT()` function for various purposes, such as extracting file extensions, working with date components, or handling codes or identifiers where the relevant information is at the end.
```

- Depending on your database system, the `RIGHT()` function might have variations in its usage, so it's a good practice to refer to your specific database's documentation for any differences in implementation.

VIII.
Handling NULL values

8.1 COALESCE()

Description:

The SQL `COALESCE()` function is used to return the first non-null expression among a list of expressions. It is a convenient way to handle situations where you have multiple values and want to select the first one that is not null.

Syntax:

The basic syntax of the `COALESCE()` function is as follows:

```sql
COALESCE(expr1, expr2, expr3, ...)
```

- `expr1, expr2, expr3, ...`: A list of expressions or values to evaluate. The function returns the first non-null expression from this list.

Example:

Suppose you have a table named `Orders` with columns `ShippedDate`, `EstimatedDeliveryDate`, and `RequiredDate`. You want to create a query that selects the first available date, whether it's the `ShippedDate`, `EstimatedDeliveryDate`, or `RequiredDate`, for each order.

```sql
SELECT OrderID, COALESCE(ShippedDate, EstimatedDeliveryDate, RequiredDate) AS FirstAvailableDate

FROM Orders;
```

Explanation of the Code:

- The SQL query selects the `OrderID` column from the `Orders` table.

- The `COALESCE()` function is applied to the three date columns (`ShippedDate`, `EstimatedDeliveryDate`, and `RequiredDate`) with the following arguments:

  - `ShippedDate`: The first expression to evaluate.

  - `EstimatedDeliveryDate`: The second expression to evaluate if the first is null.

  - `RequiredDate`: The third expression to evaluate if the first two are null.

- The result is returned as `FirstAvailableDate`, which displays the first non-null date value for each order.

Tips:

- The `COALESCE()` function is useful for handling cases where you want to find the first non-null value from a list of expressions or columns.

- You can use `COALESCE()` with different data types, such as strings, numbers, or dates, making it a versatile function for handling a wide range of scenarios.

- It's common to use `COALESCE()` with columns that may contain null values to provide a fallback value or to prioritize data from one column over others.

- When using `COALESCE()`, consider the order of the expressions you provide. The function returns the first non-null value it encounters, so order the expressions based on your preference or business logic.

- This function can improve query readability and simplify logic when you have multiple potential data sources. It's particularly useful when working with outer joins, where null values can occur.

8.2 NULLIF()

Description:

The SQL `NULLIF()` function is used to compare two expressions or values. It returns `NULL` if the two expressions are equal; otherwise, it returns the first expression. This function is particularly useful when you want to replace one value with another value if they are not equal.

Syntax:

The basic syntax of the `NULLIF()` function is as follows:

```sql
NULLIF(expr1, expr2)
```

- `expr1`: The first expression to compare.

- `expr2`: The second expression to compare. If `expr1` is equal to `expr2`, the function returns `NULL`.

Example:

Suppose you have a table named `Employees` with columns `EmployeeID`, `FirstName`, and `LastName`. You want to retrieve employee names, but if the first and last names are the same, you want to display just one of them.

```sql
SELECT EmployeeID, FirstName, NULLIF(FirstName, LastName) AS DisplayName
FROM Employees;
```

Explanation of the Code:

- The SQL query selects the `EmployeeID` and `FirstName` columns from the `Employees` table.

- The `NULLIF()` function is used to compare `FirstName` and `LastName`. If they are equal, the function returns `NULL`. If they are not equal, it returns the value of `FirstName`.

- The result is returned as `DisplayName`, which displays the first name if it's different from the last name, and `NULL` if they are the same.

Tips:

- The `NULLIF()` function is a convenient way to handle cases where you want to suppress data if it meets a specific condition.

- You can use `NULLIF()` with various data types, such as strings, numbers, or dates, to check for equality between expressions.

- It's particularly useful in cases where you want to filter or modify the display of data based on conditions without the need for complex `CASE` expressions.

- Use `NULLIF()` when you want to simplify queries by avoiding complex logic and conditional expressions.

- Remember that `NULLIF()` only returns `NULL` if the two expressions are equal; otherwise, it returns the first expression.

8.3 IFNULL()

Description:

The SQL `IFNULL()` function is used to handle `NULL` values in expressions or columns. It takes two arguments: an expression or column and a value to replace `NULL` if the expression is `NULL`. If the expression is not `NULL`, the function returns the original expression. This is particularly useful for scenarios where you want to provide a default value when a column has a `NULL` value.

Syntax:

The basic syntax of the `IFNULL()` function is as follows:

```sql
IFNULL(expr, value)
```

- `expr`: The expression or column to evaluate. If this is `NULL`, it will be replaced with the `value`.

- `value`: The value to return if `expr` is `NULL`.

Example:

Suppose you have a table named `Products` with columns `ProductID`, `ProductName`, and `Price`. You want to retrieve the product name and price, but if the price is `NULL`, you want to display a default price of 0.

```sql
SELECT ProductID, ProductName, IFNULL(Price, 0) AS DisplayPrice
FROM Products;
```

Explanation of the Code:

- The SQL query selects the `ProductID` and `ProductName` columns from the `Products` table.

- The `IFNULL()` function is used to check the `Price` column. If the `Price` is `NULL`, it replaces it with the value 0. If the `Price` is not `NULL`, it returns the original `Price`.

- The result is returned as `DisplayPrice`, which displays the original price if it's not `NULL`, and 0 if the price is `NULL`.

Tips:

- The `IFNULL()` function is a convenient way to handle `NULL` values in your SQL queries.

- It's especially useful when you want to ensure that your result set doesn't contain `NULL` values and can replace them with default values.

- You can use `IFNULL()` with various data types, including numbers, strings, and dates.

- Be mindful of the data types when specifying the replacement value (`value`) to ensure compatibility.

- Similar functions like `COALESCE()` can also be used for handling `NULL` values, but `IFNULL()` is specifically designed for two arguments, making it simple and effective for this purpose.

8.4 NVL()

Description:

The SQL `NVL()` function is used to handle `NULL` values in expressions or columns, similar to `IFNULL()` in some database systems. It takes two arguments: an expression or column and a value to replace `NULL` if the expression is `NULL`. If the expression is not `NULL`, the function returns the original expression. This is particularly useful for scenarios where you want to provide a default value when a column has a `NULL` value.

Syntax:

The basic syntax of the `NVL()` function is as follows:

```sql
NVL(expr, value)
```

- `expr`: The expression or column to evaluate. If this is `NULL`, it will be replaced with the `value`.

- `value`: The value to return if `expr` is `NULL`.

Example:

Suppose you have a table named `Employees` with columns `EmployeeID`, `FirstName`, and `LastName`. You want to retrieve the full name, but if the last name is `NULL`, you want to display "N/A" as the default.

```sql
SELECT EmployeeID, FirstName, NVL(LastName, 'N/A') AS FullName

FROM Employees;
```

Explanation of the Code:

- The SQL query selects the `EmployeeID` and `FirstName` columns from the `Employees` table.

- The `NVL()` function is used to check the `LastName` column. If the `LastName` is `NULL`, it replaces it with the value "N/A." If the `LastName` is not `NULL`, it returns the original `LastName`.

- The result is returned as `FullName`, which displays "N/A" if the last name is `NULL` and the actual last name if it's not `NULL`.

Tips:

- The `NVL()` function is a convenient way to handle `NULL` values in your SQL queries, especially in Oracle databases.

- It's especially useful when you want to ensure that your result set doesn't contain `NULL` values and can replace them with default values.

- You can use `NVL()` with various data types, including strings, numbers, and dates.

- Be mindful of the data types when specifying the replacement value (`value`) to ensure compatibility.

- Depending on the database system, you might use `IFNULL()` or other similar functions for handling `NULL` values. `NVL()` is specific to Oracle databases.

8.5 IFNULL() / ISNULL()

Description:

The SQL `IFNULL()` and `ISNULL()` functions are used to handle `NULL` values in expressions or columns by providing a default value. Both functions are similar, but they are often used in different database systems.

- `IFNULL()` is commonly associated with MySQL.

- `ISNULL()` is commonly associated with Microsoft SQL Server.

These functions take two arguments: an expression or column and a value to replace `NULL` if the expression is `NULL`. If the expression is not `NULL`, the function returns the original expression. These functions are especially useful for scenarios where you want to provide a default value when a column has a `NULL` value.

Syntax:

The basic syntax of the `IFNULL()` and `ISNULL()` functions is as follows:

For MySQL (IFNULL):

```sql
IFNULL(expr, value)
```

For Microsoft SQL Server (ISNULL):

```sql
ISNULL(expr, value)
```

- `expr`: The expression or column to evaluate. If this is `NULL`, it will be replaced with the `value`.

- `value`: The value to return if `expr` is `NULL`.

Examples:

MySQL (IFNULL):

Suppose you have a table named `Orders` with columns `OrderID`, `OrderDate`, and `ShippedDate`. You want to retrieve the order date, but if it's `NULL`, you want to display "Not Shipped" as the default.

```sql
SELECT OrderID, IFNULL(OrderDate, 'Not Shipped') AS OrderStatus
FROM Orders;
```

Explanation of the Code (MySQL):

- The SQL query selects the `OrderID` column from the `Orders` table.

- The `IFNULL()` function is used to check the `OrderDate` column. If the `OrderDate` is `NULL`, it replaces it with the value "Not Shipped." If the `OrderDate` is not `NULL`, it returns the original `OrderDate`.

- The result is returned as `OrderStatus`, which displays "Not Shipped" if the order date is `NULL` and the actual order date if it's not `NULL`.

Microsoft SQL Server (ISNULL):

Suppose you have a similar table named `Orders` and want to achieve the same result:

```sql
SELECT OrderID, ISNULL(OrderDate, 'Not Shipped') AS OrderStatus
FROM Orders;
```

Tips:

- The `IFNULL()` and `ISNULL()` functions are convenient ways to handle `NULL` values in your SQL queries, commonly used in MySQL and Microsoft SQL Server, respectively.

- They are especially useful when you want to ensure that your result set doesn't contain `NULL` values and can replace them with default values.

- You can use `IFNULL()` or `ISNULL()` with various data types, including strings, numbers, and dates.

- Be mindful of the data types when specifying the replacement value (`value`) to ensure compatibility.

- Depending on the database system you're using, you should choose `IFNULL()` or `ISNULL()` accordingly.

8.6 CASE WHEN... THEN... ELSE... END

Description:

The SQL `CASE` statement is a conditional expression that allows you to perform conditional logic in your SQL queries. You can use it to evaluate a set of conditions and return a corresponding result based on the first condition that is met.

Syntax:

The basic syntax of the `CASE` statement is as follows:

```sql
CASE
    WHEN condition1 THEN result1
    WHEN condition2 THEN result2
    ...
    ELSE else_result
END
```

- `condition1`, `condition2`, etc.: These are the conditions to be evaluated. If a condition is true, the corresponding result is returned.

- `result1`, `result2`, etc.: These are the values or expressions to return if the corresponding condition is true.

- `else_result`: This is the value or expression to return if none of the conditions is true (optional).

Examples:

Suppose you have a table named `Students` with columns `FirstName`, `LastName`, and `Grade`, and you want to categorize students based on their grades into "Excellent," "Good," "Satisfactory," and "Needs Improvement." You can use the `CASE` statement for this purpose:

```sql
SELECT FirstName, LastName, Grade,
   CASE
       WHEN Grade >= 90 THEN 'Excellent'
       WHEN Grade >= 80 THEN 'Good'
       WHEN Grade >= 70 THEN 'Satisfactory'
       ELSE 'Needs Improvement'
   END AS GradeCategory
FROM Students;
```

Explanation of the Code:

- The SQL query selects `FirstName`, `LastName`, and `Grade` columns from the `Students` table.

- The `CASE` statement evaluates the `Grade` column against multiple conditions.

- If `Grade` is greater than or equal to 90, the result is 'Excellent.'

- If `Grade` is greater than or equal to 80, the result is 'Good.'

- If `Grade` is greater than or equal to 70, the result is 'Satisfactory.'

- If none of the conditions are met (i.e., `Grade` is less than 70), the result is 'Needs Improvement.'

- The results are returned as `GradeCategory`.

Tips:

- The `CASE` statement is a powerful tool for performing conditional operations within your SQL queries.

- You can use it not only in the `SELECT` statement but also in other SQL statements like `UPDATE` and `INSERT`.

- The conditions within the `CASE` statement are evaluated in order, and the first condition that is true will determine the result. So, order your conditions carefully.

- If you want to provide a default result when none of the conditions are met, you can use the `ELSE` clause. This part is optional, but it's a good practice to include it for handling unexpected cases.

IX.
Aggregate functions

9.1 GROUP_CONCAT() / STRING_AGG()

Description:

The SQL `GROUP_CONCAT()` function, which is known as `STRING_AGG()` in some database systems, is an aggregate function that is used to concatenate values from multiple rows into a single string. It is particularly useful when you want to combine values from multiple rows based on a common attribute, typically when using the `GROUP BY` clause.

Syntax:

The syntax of the `GROUP_CONCAT()` function (or `STRING_AGG()`) is as follows:

```sql
GROUP_CONCAT(column_name [ORDER BY order_column] [SEPARATOR 'separator'])
```

- `column_name`: The name of the column you want to concatenate.

- `ORDER BY order_column` (optional): Specifies the order in which values from `column_name` are concatenated. This is often used when the order of the concatenated values matters.

- `SEPARATOR 'separator'` (optional): Defines the separator between concatenated values. The default separator is a comma (`,`).

Examples:

Suppose you have a table named `Orders` with columns `OrderID`, `Product`, and `CustomerID`, and you want to concatenate the product names for each customer. You can use the `GROUP_CONCAT()` function in MySQL or the `STRING_AGG()` function in SQL Server:

```sql
-- MySQL (using GROUP_CONCAT)
SELECT CustomerID, GROUP_CONCAT(Product ORDER BY OrderID) AS Products
FROM Orders
GROUP BY CustomerID;
```

```sql
-- SQL Server (using STRING_AGG)
SELECT CustomerID, STRING_AGG(Product, ', ') AS Products
FROM Orders
GROUP BY CustomerID;
```

Explanation of the Code:

- The SQL query selects `CustomerID` and uses the `GROUP_CONCAT()` or `STRING_AGG()` function to concatenate the `Product` column.

- In MySQL, the `ORDER BY` clause is used to specify that the products should be ordered by the `OrderID`.

- The `GROUP BY` clause groups the result by `CustomerID`.

- The result is a list of products for each customer.

Tips:

- The `GROUP_CONCAT()` function is available in MySQL and some other database systems.

- In SQL Server, you can use the `STRING_AGG()` function to achieve the same result.

- The `ORDER BY` clause is optional but can be useful for controlling the order of concatenated values.

- You can change the default separator (`,` in most cases) by specifying the `SEPARATOR` parameter. This allows you to customize the format of the concatenated string.

- The `GROUP_CONCAT()` or `STRING_AGG()` function is very useful for generating comma-separated lists or any other delimited strings from grouped data, which is a common requirement in SQL reporting and data analysis.

9.2 GROUPING()

Description:

The SQL `GROUPING()` function is used in conjunction with the `GROUP BY` clause to identify whether a specific column is part of the grouping set. This function is commonly used in scenarios where grouping sets or roll-up operations are involved. It returns a value indicating whether a column is part of the grouping set.

Syntax:

The syntax for the `GROUPING()` function is as follows:

```sql
GROUPING(column_name)
```

- `column_name`: The name of the column that you want to check within the grouping set.

Examples:

Consider a table named `Sales` with columns `Region`, `Year`, and `SalesAmount`. You want to perform a roll-up operation to find the total sales amount for each region, and you also want to know whether the result is at the "Region" level or the "Year" level.

Here's how you can use the `GROUP BY` clause with `GROUPING()` to achieve this in SQL:

```sql
SELECT
    Region,
    Year,
    SUM(SalesAmount) AS TotalSales,
    GROUPING(Region) AS IsRegionGrouping,
    GROUPING(Year) AS IsYearGrouping
FROM Sales
GROUP BY ROLLUP (Region, Year)
ORDER BY Region, Year;
```

Explanation of the Code:

- The SQL query selects `Region`, `Year`, and the total `SalesAmount`.

- The `GROUPING(Region)` and `GROUPING(Year)` functions are used to determine if the current row is at the "Region" or "Year" level of grouping. These functions return `1` when the column is part of the grouping set and `0` when it is not.

- The `ROLLUP` clause is used in the `GROUP BY` clause to perform the roll-up operation, which generates subtotals for each level of grouping (in this case, for "Region" and "Year").

- The `ORDER BY` clause orders the result by `Region` and `Year`.

Tips:

- The `GROUPING()` function is commonly used with roll-up and cube operations in SQL to identify the level of aggregation in the result set.

- It is helpful when you want to determine whether a specific column is part of the grouping set, especially in scenarios where multiple levels of grouping are involved.

- The function returns `1` if the column is part of the grouping set, and `0` if it is not.

- Using `GROUPING()` can help you create more informative summary reports or pivot tables with different levels of aggregation.

9.3 STDEV() / STDDEV()

Description:

The SQL `STDEV()` (or `STDDEV()`) function calculates the standard deviation of a set of values in a given dataset. The standard deviation is a measure of how spread out or dispersed the values in a dataset are. It quantifies the amount of variation or uncertainty in the data. A low standard deviation indicates that the data points tend to be close to the mean, while a high standard deviation indicates that the data points are more spread out.

Syntax:

The syntax for the `STDEV()` function is as follows:

```sql
STDEV(column_name)
```

- `column_name`: The name of the column or expression for which you want to calculate the standard deviation.

Example Usage:

Consider a table named `Scores` with a column named `Score` that contains exam scores. You want to find the standard deviation of the exam scores.

Here's how you can use the `STDEV()` function in SQL:

```sql
SELECT STDEV(Score) AS StandardDeviation
FROM Scores;
```

Explanation of the Code:

- The SQL query calculates the standard deviation of the `Score` column in the `Scores` table using the `STDEV()` function.

- The result of this query will be a single value representing the standard deviation of the exam scores.

Tips:

- The standard deviation is a useful statistical measure to understand the variability of data. A lower standard deviation indicates that data points are closer to the mean, while a higher standard deviation suggests greater dispersion.

- The `STDEV()` function can be used in various scenarios, such as in quality control, finance, and data analysis, to measure data variability.

- Be sure to understand the nature of your dataset and the context in which you are using the standard deviation. In some cases, it may be appropriate to calculate the population standard deviation (using all data points) or the sample standard deviation (using a subset of data points). SQL provides functions for both scenarios (`STDEVP()` for population standard deviation and `STDEV()` for sample standard deviation).

- When using the `STDEV()` function, ensure that your dataset is representative of the population you want to analyze. If you're working with a sample, consider the implications of using a sample standard deviation versus a population standard deviation.

9.4 VAR() / VARIANCE()

Description:

The SQL `VAR()` (or `VARIANCE()`) function is used to calculate the variance of a set of values within a given dataset. Variance is a statistical measure that quantifies the degree of spread or dispersion in a dataset. It provides insight into how individual data points deviate from the dataset's mean. A low variance indicates that data points are close to the mean, while a high variance suggests that data points are more spread out.

Syntax:

The syntax for the `VAR()` function is as follows:

```sql
VAR(column_name)
```

- `column_name`: The name of the column or expression for which you want to calculate the variance.

Example Usage:

Let's consider a table named `SalaryData` with a column named `Salary` that contains salary information for employees. You want to find the variance of the salaries in this dataset.

Here's how you can use the `VAR()` function in SQL:

```sql
SELECT VAR(Salary) AS SalaryVariance
FROM SalaryData;
```

Explanation of the Code:

- The SQL query calculates the variance of the `Salary` column in the `SalaryData` table using the `VAR()` function.

- The result of this query will be a single value representing the variance of the employee salaries.

Tips:

- Variance is a valuable statistical measure for understanding data variability. It's used in various fields, including finance, quality control, and data analysis.

- Variance can be affected by outliers or extreme values. If your dataset contains outliers that significantly impact the variance calculation, you might consider using other measures, such as the interquartile range (IQR) or a trimmed mean, to assess data spread.

- Make sure to understand whether you need the population variance (using all data points) or the sample variance (using a subset of data points). SQL provides functions for both scenarios (`VARP()` for population variance and `VAR()` for sample variance).

- When using the `VAR()` function, consider the nature of your dataset and the context in which you're analyzing it. The choice of statistical measures should align with your specific objectives and data characteristics.

9.5 MEDIAN()

Description:

The SQL `MEDIAN()` function is used to calculate the median of a set of values within a given dataset. The median is a statistical measure that represents the middle value of a dataset when it is ordered. It is especially useful when dealing with datasets that may contain outliers or when you want to find the central tendency of your data.

Syntax:

The syntax for the `MEDIAN()` function is as follows:

```sql
MEDIAN(column_name)
```

- `column_name`: The name of the column or expression for which you want to calculate the median.

Example Usage:

Let's consider a table named `TestScores` with a column named `Score` that contains test scores for students. You want to find the median test score in this dataset.

Here's how you can use the `MEDIAN()` function in SQL:

```sql
SELECT MEDIAN(Score) AS MedianScore
FROM TestScores;
```

Explanation of the Code:

- The SQL query calculates the median of the `Score` column in the `TestScores` table using the `MEDIAN()` function.

- The result of this query will be a single value representing the median test score.

Tips:

- The median is a robust measure of central tendency because it is not affected by extreme values (outliers) in the dataset. This makes it a useful choice when working with data that may have significant outliers.

- In SQL, the availability of the `MEDIAN()` function may depend on the database system you are using. Not all database management systems support this function natively. In such cases, you might need to use custom queries or statistical techniques to calculate the median.

- When dealing with datasets that have an odd number of values, the median is the middle value. In datasets with an even number of values, the median is typically calculated as the average of the two middle values.

- If the dataset contains a large number of rows, consider whether you want to calculate the median over the entire dataset or for specific groups or categories. You can use the `GROUP BY` clause to calculate medians for different groups if needed.

- Ensure that your dataset is correctly sorted before calculating the median using the `ORDER BY` clause if necessary. The median relies on sorted data to determine the middle value.

- The median is particularly useful for datasets that do not follow a normal distribution, where the mean might not be an appropriate measure of central tendency.

9.6 MODE()

Description:

The SQL `MODE()` function, sometimes referred to as `MODUS()`, is used to calculate the mode of a set of values within a given dataset. The mode is a statistical measure that represents the most frequently occurring value in a dataset. It can be useful for identifying the most common element in a dataset, which can be helpful in various analytical and reporting scenarios.

Syntax:

The syntax for the `MODE()` function is not standard in SQL and may vary depending on the database system you are using. The following illustrates a common way to calculate the mode:

```sql
SELECT column_name, COUNT(column_name) AS mode_count
FROM table_name
GROUP BY column_name
ORDER BY COUNT(column_name) DESC
LIMIT 1;
```

- `column_name`: The name of the column for which you want to find the mode.

- `table_name`: The name of the table that contains the dataset.

Example Usage:

Suppose you have a table named `Sales` with a column named `ProductCategory`, and you want to find the mode (most common product category) from this dataset.

Here's how you can use the `MODE()` function in SQL:

```sql
SELECT ProductCategory, COUNT(ProductCategory) AS mode_count

FROM Sales

GROUP BY ProductCategory

ORDER BY COUNT(ProductCategory) DESC

LIMIT 1;
```

Explanation of the Code:

- The SQL query calculates the mode by grouping the data by the `ProductCategory` column.

- It counts the occurrences of each product category using the `COUNT()` function and gives it an alias `mode_count`.

- The result set is then ordered in descending order of the `mode_count` to identify the most frequent value.

- The `LIMIT 1` clause ensures that only the first row (the mode) is returned.

Tips:

- The mode is particularly useful when you want to identify the most common or popular element in a dataset. For example, it can help you find the most popular product, the most common symptom in a medical dataset, or the most frequent category in sales data.

- SQL does not have a built-in `MODE()` function like it does for `SUM()`, `AVG()`, or `COUNT()`. Therefore, you need to use custom SQL queries, as shown in the example, to calculate the mode.

- Be aware that there can be multiple modes in a dataset, especially if more than one value has the same highest frequency. In the SQL example provided, the query returns only one mode, but you might need to modify it to identify multiple modes if necessary.

- If you expect there to be multiple modes and want to retrieve all of them, you can omit the `LIMIT 1` clause. This will return all values with the highest frequency.

- When dealing with large datasets, be aware of the performance implications of using the `GROUP BY` clause and aggregating functions like `COUNT()`. Indexing and data distribution can significantly impact the query's speed.

- Always make sure that your dataset is correctly structured and organized. Inconsistent or missing data can affect the accuracy of mode calculations.

9.7 CORR()

Description:

The SQL `CORR()` function, sometimes referred to as `CORRELATION()`, is used to calculate the correlation coefficient between two sets of values within a dataset. The correlation coefficient is a statistical measure that quantifies the strength and direction of a linear relationship between two variables. It is often used to determine how changes in one variable are related to changes in another. The result can range from -1 to 1, where -1 indicates a perfect negative correlation, 1 indicates a perfect positive correlation, and 0 indicates no correlation.

Syntax:

The syntax for the `CORR()` function may vary depending on the specific database system you are using. Here is a general representation:

```sql
CORR(column1, column2)
```

- `column1`: The name of the first column you want to calculate the correlation for.

- `column2`: The name of the second column you want to calculate the correlation with.

Example Usage:

Suppose you have a table named `StudentGrades` with two columns, `MathScore` and `PhysicsScore`, and you want to find the correlation between the math scores and physics scores of students.

Here's how you can use the `CORR()` function in SQL:

```sql
SELECT CORR(MathScore, PhysicsScore) AS correlation

FROM StudentGrades;
```

Explanation of the Code:

- The SQL query calculates the correlation between the `MathScore` and `PhysicsScore` columns using the `CORR()` function.

- It assigns an alias `correlation` to the result.

- The query will return a numerical value representing the correlation coefficient between the two columns. This value can range from -1 (perfect negative correlation) to 1 (perfect positive correlation), with 0 indicating no correlation.

Tips:

- The correlation coefficient is a useful measure for understanding the relationship between two variables. For example, in business, it can help determine whether there is a correlation between advertising spending and sales revenue. In health, it can be used to investigate the correlation between two health indicators.

- A positive correlation means that as one variable increases, the other tends to increase as well. A negative correlation indicates that as one variable increases, the other tends to decrease. A correlation of 0 suggests that there is no linear relationship between the two variables.

- Keep in mind that correlation does not imply causation. Even if two variables are highly correlated, it doesn't mean that one variable causes the other. Other factors or variables may be involved.

- When interpreting correlation coefficients, a value close to -1 or 1 indicates a strong relationship, while a value close to 0 suggests a weak relationship. However, a low correlation coefficient doesn't necessarily mean that the variables are unrelated; they may have a nonlinear relationship.

- Ensure that your dataset is clean and free from missing or erroneous data, as outliers and missing values can distort the correlation coefficient.

- Be cautious when interpreting correlation results, especially in cases where outliers may unduly influence the correlation coefficient. Outliers can artificially inflate or deflate correlation values.

9.8 COVAR_POP()

Description:

The SQL `COVAR_POP()` function, short for "covariance of the population," is used to calculate the covariance between two sets of values within a dataset. Covariance measures how two variables change together, indicating whether they have a positive or negative relationship. It provides information about the direction of the linear relationship between two variables. Positive covariance suggests that when one variable is above its mean, the other tends to be above its mean as well, and vice versa for negative covariance.

The formula for `COVAR_POP()` is as follows:

```
COVAR_POP(X, Y) = Σ [(Xᵢ - μ(X)) * (Yᵢ - μ(Y))] / N
```

$$COVAR\_POP(X, Y) = \Sigma\, [(X_i - \mu(X)) * (Y_i - \mu(Y))] / N$$

Where:

- `X` and `Y` are the two variables for which you want to calculate the covariance.

- `Xᵢ` and `Yᵢ` are individual data points.

- `μ(X)` and `μ(Y)` are the means of `X` and `Y`, respectively.

- `N` is the number of data points.

The result of `COVAR_POP()` is expressed in the units of the product of the units of the two variables being measured.

Syntax:

The syntax for the `COVAR_POP()` function may vary depending on the specific database system you are using. Here is a general representation:

```sql
COVAR_POP(column1, column2)
```

- `column1`: The name of the first column for which you want to calculate the covariance.
- `column2`: The name of the second column for which you want to calculate the covariance.

Example Usage:

Suppose you have a table named `StockPrices` with two columns, `PriceA` and `PriceB`, and you want to calculate the population covariance between the prices of stock A and stock B.

Here's how you can use the `COVAR_POP()` function in SQL:

```sql
SELECT COVAR_POP(PriceA, PriceB) AS covariance
FROM StockPrices;
```

Explanation of the Code:

- The SQL query calculates the covariance between the `PriceA` and `PriceB` columns using the `COVAR_POP()` function.

- It assigns an alias `covariance` to the result.

- The query will return a numerical value representing the covariance between the two columns. The value can be positive or negative, indicating the direction of the relationship between the two variables.

Tips:

- Covariance measures the degree to which two variables change together, but it doesn't provide a standardized measure of the strength of their relationship. Correlation coefficients, such as the Pearson correlation coefficient, are more commonly used to measure the strength and direction of a linear relationship.

- A positive covariance suggests that as one variable increases, the other variable tends to increase, while a negative covariance suggests that as one variable increases, the other variable tends to decrease.

- Be cautious when interpreting covariance values, as they are not normalized and can be influenced by the scale of the variables. To compare the strength of relationships between different pairs of variables, it is often more appropriate to use correlation coefficients.

- Ensure that your dataset is clean and free from missing or erroneous data, as outliers and missing values can significantly affect covariance results.

- Keep in mind that covariance is sensitive to units of measurement. Converting variables to standardized scores (z-scores) can make covariance results more meaningful and interpretable.

9.9 COVAR_SAMP()

Description:

The SQL `COVAR_SAMP()` function, short for "sample covariance," is used to calculate the covariance between two sets of values within a dataset. Covariance measures how two variables change together, indicating whether they have a positive or negative relationship. It provides information about the direction of the linear relationship between two variables. Positive covariance suggests that when one variable is above its mean, the other tends to be above its mean as well, and vice versa for negative covariance.

`COVAR_SAMP()` is used when you want to calculate the covariance based on a sample of data. It is an estimator of the population covariance and is used when you have a subset (sample) of the data and you want to estimate the covariance between variables for the entire population.

The formula for `COVAR_SAMP()` is as follows:

```
COVAR_SAMP(X, Y) = Σ [(Xi - x̄) * (Yi - ȳ)] / (n - 1)
```

Where:

- `X` and `Y` are the two variables for which you want to calculate the covariance.

- `Xᵢ` and `Yᵢ` are individual data points.

- `x̄` and `ȳ` are the sample means of `X` and `Y`, respectively.

- `n` is the number of data points in the sample.

The result of `COVAR_SAMP()` is expressed in the units of the product of the units of the two variables being measured.

Syntax:

The syntax for the `COVAR_SAMP()` function may vary depending on the specific database system you are using. Here is a general representation:

```sql
COVAR_SAMP(column1, column2)
```

- `column1`: The name of the first column for which you want to calculate the covariance.
- `column2`: The name of the second column for which you want to calculate the covariance.

Example Usage:

Suppose you have a table named `StockPrices` with two columns, `PriceA` and `PriceB`, and you want to calculate the sample covariance between the prices of stock A and stock B for a specific sample.

Here's how you can use the `COVAR_SAMP()` function in SQL:

```sql
```

```
SELECT COVAR_SAMP(PriceA, PriceB) AS sample_covariance

FROM StockPrices

WHERE Date BETWEEN '2023-01-01' AND '2023-12-31';
```

Explanation of the Code:

- The SQL query calculates the sample covariance between the `PriceA` and `PriceB` columns using the `COVAR_SAMP()` function.

- It assigns an alias `sample_covariance` to the result.

- The `WHERE` clause restricts the calculation to a specific sample of data, in this case, data within a particular date range.

- The query will return a numerical value representing the sample covariance between the two columns. The value can be positive or negative, indicating the direction of the relationship between the two variables in the sample.

Tips:

- Covariance measures the degree to which two variables change together but doesn't provide a standardized measure of the strength of their relationship. Correlation coefficients, such as the Pearson correlation coefficient, are more commonly used to measure the strength and direction of a linear relationship.

- The use of `COVAR_SAMP()` assumes that the sample is a representative subset of the population, and it provides an unbiased estimate of the population covariance. However, with smaller samples, estimates may be less reliable.

- Be cautious when interpreting covariance values, as they are not normalized and can be influenced by the scale of the variables. To compare the strength of relationships between different pairs of variables, it is often more appropriate to use correlation coefficients.

- Ensure that your dataset is clean and free from missing or erroneous data, as outliers and missing values can significantly affect covariance results.

- Keep in mind that covariance is sensitive to units of measurement. Converting variables to standardized scores (z-scores) can make covariance results more meaningful and interpretable.

9.10 PERCENTILE_CONT()

Description:

The SQL `PERCENTILE_CONT()` function is used to calculate the value at a specific percentile within a set of values in a dataset. It provides a way to find a value that separates a distribution of values into two parts, with a certain proportion of values falling below that value. This function is particularly useful for analyzing data distributions, understanding data spread, and identifying data points at specific percentiles.

The `PERCENTILE_CONT()` function calculates the value at the specified percentile using linear interpolation. This means that it estimates the value by finding the two closest data points, calculating a weighted average between them based on the given percentile, and returning the estimated value. This method is commonly used in statistics to estimate percentiles.

Syntax:

The syntax for the `PERCENTILE_CONT()` function is as follows:

```sql
PERCENTILE_CONT(percentile) WITHIN GROUP (ORDER BY column)
```

- `percentile`: A numeric value between 0 and 1, representing the desired percentile (e.g., 0.25 for the 25th percentile).

- `column`: The column containing the values for which you want to find the percentile.

Example Usage:

Suppose you have a table named `ExamScores` with a column named `Score` containing exam scores, and you want to find the value at the 75th percentile.

Here's how you can use the `PERCENTILE_CONT()` function in SQL:

```sql
SELECT PERCENTILE_CONT(0.75) WITHIN GROUP (ORDER BY Score) AS percentile_value
FROM ExamScores;
```

Explanation of the Code:

- The SQL query calculates the value at the 75th percentile of the `Score` column using the `PERCENTILE_CONT()` function.

- It assigns an alias `percentile_value` to the result.

- The `ORDER BY` clause is used to specify the order in which the data should be sorted. In this case, it sorts the data by the `Score` column in ascending order.

- The query will return a numerical value that represents the value at the 75th percentile of the exam scores in the dataset.

Tips:

- Ensure that the column you are using with the `PERCENTILE_CONT()` function contains numeric or ordered data, as this function relies on sorting and interpolation.

- The `percentile` parameter should be a numeric value between 0 and 1, where 0 represents the minimum value, 1 represents the maximum value, and values in between represent the desired percentiles.

- The function calculates the estimated value at the specified percentile using linear interpolation. If the data contains a large number of values, the result is likely to be close to one of the actual data points, but it may not match exactly.

- Be aware that there are different methods for calculating percentiles in statistics, such as linear interpolation, nearest rank, and exclusive percentiles. Ensure that the `PERCENTILE_CONT()` function's behavior matches your specific requirements.

- If you want to find multiple percentiles in a single query, you can use multiple `PERCENTILE_CONT()` functions with different `percentile` values.

- This function is especially useful for exploring the spread of data and identifying values that correspond to specific percentiles, such as quartiles or median.

9.11 PERCENTILE_DISC()

Description:

The SQL `PERCENTILE_DISC()` function is used to calculate the discrete percentile (or exact percentile) within a set of values in a dataset. It provides a way to find a value that separates a distribution of values into two parts, with a certain proportion of values falling below that value. This function is particularly useful for finding the exact value at specific percentiles in a dataset.

Unlike the `PERCENTILE_CONT()` function, which uses linear interpolation to estimate percentiles, `PERCENTILE_DISC()` returns an exact value from the dataset. It is useful when you need to find the value that corresponds to a specific percentile without estimating it.

Syntax:

The syntax for the `PERCENTILE_DISC()` function is as follows:

```sql
PERCENTILE_DISC(percentile) WITHIN GROUP (ORDER BY column)
```

- `percentile`: A numeric value between 0 and 1, representing the desired percentile (e.g., 0.25 for the 25th percentile).

- `column`: The column containing the values for which you want to find the percentile.

Example Usage:

Suppose you have a table named `Income` with a column named `Salary` containing income data, and you want to find the exact value at the 90th percentile.

Here's how you can use the `PERCENTILE_DISC()` function in SQL:

```sql
SELECT PERCENTILE_DISC(0.9) WITHIN GROUP (ORDER BY Salary) AS percentile_value
FROM Income;
```

Explanation of the Code:

- The SQL query calculates the value at the 90th percentile of the `Salary` column using the `PERCENTILE_DISC()` function.

- It assigns an alias `percentile_value` to the result.

- The `ORDER BY` clause is used to specify the order in which the data should be sorted. In this case, it sorts the data by the `Salary` column in ascending order.

- The query will return the exact value that corresponds to the 90th percentile of the income data in the dataset.

Tips:

- Ensure that the column you are using with the `PERCENTILE_DISC()` function contains numeric or ordered data, as this function relies on sorting the data.

- The `percentile` parameter should be a numeric value between 0 and 1, where 0 represents the minimum value, 1 represents the maximum value, and values in between represent the desired percentiles.

- Unlike `PERCENTILE_CONT()`, `PERCENTILE_DISC()` returns an exact value from the dataset. It is particularly useful when you need to find values that match specific percentiles without interpolation.

- Be aware that there are different methods for calculating percentiles in statistics, such as linear interpolation, nearest rank, and discrete percentiles. Ensure that the `PERCENTILE_DISC()` function's behavior matches your specific requirements.

- If you want to find multiple percentiles in a single query, you can use multiple `PERCENTILE_DISC()` functions with different `percentile` values.

- This function is especially useful for finding exact values that correspond to specific percentiles, such as quartiles or median, when dealing with discrete data.

9.12 RANK()

Description:

The SQL `RANK()` function is used to assign a rank to each row within the result set of a query. It is a window function that assigns a unique rank to each row based on the values in one or more columns. Rows with the same values receive the same rank, and the next rank is skipped. This function is commonly used in analytical and reporting queries when you need to identify the rank of rows based on specific criteria.

Syntax:

The syntax for the `RANK()` function is as follows:

```sql
RANK() OVER (PARTITION BY column1, column2,... ORDER BY columnA, columnB,...)
```

- `PARTITION BY column1, column2, ...`: This is an optional clause that divides the result set into partitions. The `RANK()` function assigns ranks separately within each partition.

- `ORDER BY columnA, columnB, ...`: This clause specifies the columns by which the ranking is determined. Rows are ranked in ascending order by default, but you can specify descending order using the `DESC` keyword.

Example Usage:

Suppose you have a table named `Students` with columns `StudentID`, `Score`, and `Subject`. You want to rank students based on their scores in each subject.

Here's how you can use the `RANK()` function in SQL:

```sql
SELECT StudentID, Score, Subject, RANK() OVER (PARTITION BY Subject ORDER BY Score DESC) AS Rank

FROM Students;
```

Explanation of the Code:

- The SQL query retrieves the `StudentID`, `Score`, and `Subject` columns from the `Students` table.

- It uses the `RANK()` function to assign a rank to each student's score within each subject. The `PARTITION BY Subject` clause ensures that ranking is done separately for each subject.

- The `ORDER BY Score DESC` clause specifies that rows should be ranked in descending order of scores.

- The query will return a result set with the student's ID, score, subject, and their rank within the subject based on their scores.

Tips:

- The `RANK()` function is often used with the `PARTITION BY` clause to rank rows within specific groups or categories. This is useful when you want to calculate rankings independently for each group.

- If you want to handle ties, where rows with the same values receive the same rank and the next rank is skipped, you can use the `DENSE_RANK()` function instead. `DENSE_RANK()` assigns consecutive ranks to tied rows.

- In cases where you don't need consecutive ranks for tied values and want to skip the next rank after a tie, the `RANK()` function is suitable.

- The `ORDER BY` clause specifies the columns by which ranking is determined. You can specify multiple columns and their order (ascending or descending) to define the ranking criteria.

- Use window functions like `RANK()` in analytical queries to gain insights into your data, such as identifying the top performers, identifying outliers, or segmenting data by rank.

- Window functions are supported in most modern SQL database management systems, including PostgreSQL, MySQL, SQL Server, and Oracle. However, the syntax may vary slightly between systems.

9.13 NTILE()

Description:

The SQL `NTILE()` function is a window function used to divide the result set into a specified number of roughly equal parts or "tiles" and assign a tile number to each row within those partitions. It is commonly used for data analysis, especially in scenarios where you need to categorize data into percentiles or quartiles.

Syntax:

The syntax for the `NTILE()` function is as follows:

```sql
NTILE(number_of_tiles) OVER (PARTITION BY column1, column2,... ORDER BY columnA, columnB,...)
```

- `number_of_tiles`: The total number of tiles or partitions you want the result set to be divided into.

- `PARTITION BY column1, column2, ...`: This is an optional clause that divides the result set into partitions. The `NTILE()` function assigns tile numbers separately within each partition.

- `ORDER BY columnA, columnB, ...`: This clause specifies the columns by which the order of rows is determined.

Example Usage:

Suppose you have a table named `Sales` with columns `Region` and `Revenue`, and you want to divide the sales data into quartiles based on revenue for each region.

Here's how you can use the `NTILE()` function in SQL:

```sql
SELECT Region, Revenue, NTILE(4) OVER (PARTITION BY Region ORDER BY Revenue) AS Quartile

FROM Sales;
```

Explanation of the Code:

- The SQL query retrieves the `Region`, `Revenue`, and `NTILE(4) OVER ...` columns from the `Sales` table.

- It uses the `NTILE()` function to divide the sales data into four quartiles based on the `Revenue` column within each `Region`.

- The `PARTITION BY Region` clause ensures that quartiles are calculated separately for each region.

- The `ORDER BY Revenue` clause specifies that rows should be ordered by revenue.

- The query returns a result set with the region, revenue, and the quartile to which each sale belongs based on revenue.

Tips:

- The `NTILE()` function is typically used to divide data into equal parts. For example, when you use `NTILE(4)`, it divides data into quartiles, or `NTILE(100)` can be used to divide data into percentiles.

- Use the `PARTITION BY` clause to perform calculations within specific groups or categories. This is useful when you want to divide data into percentiles or quartiles within distinct groups.

- The `ORDER BY` clause specifies the column by which the order of rows is determined. This column is typically used to calculate percentiles or quartiles.

- You can choose the number of tiles based on your specific requirements. For quartiles, use `NTILE(4)`; for quintiles, use `NTILE(5)`, and so on.

- The `NTILE()` function is valuable in data analysis and reporting when you need to categorize data into segments based on specific criteria, such as revenue, scores, or other numerical values.

- Window functions like `NTILE()` are supported in most modern SQL database management systems, including PostgreSQL, MySQL, SQL Server, and Oracle. However, the syntax may vary slightly between systems.

CONCLUSION

In conclusion, SQL functions play a crucial role in database management and data processing. These functions allow you to perform a wide range of operations on data, from simple tasks like arithmetic calculations and text manipulations to more advanced tasks such as statistical analysis and date transformations. By using SQL functions effectively, you can streamline your queries, ensure data integrity, and gain insights from your data.

Throughout this series of explanations, we've covered various SQL functions, including mathematical, string, date, and aggregate functions, providing you with detailed descriptions, syntax, examples, and tips for each function. We hope these explanations have been helpful in your journey to mastering SQL.

Thank You:

We would like to express our gratitude to you, our readers, for taking the time to explore SQL functions with us. Your curiosity and desire to learn are what drive us to provide informative and comprehensive content. If you have any more questions or need assistance with any other topics, please feel free to ask. We're here to help you on your learning journey.

Happy querying and data management!